# FAITH LESSONS

## ON THE prophets & KINGS OF ISRAEL

# LEADER'S GUIDE

## Ray Vander Laan

with

Stephen and Amanda Sorenson

ZondervanPublishingHouse

*Grand Rapids, Michigan*

*A Division of HarperCollinsPublishers*

*Faith Lessons on the Prophets and Kings of Israel Leader's Guide*

Copyright © 1999 by Ray Vander Laan

Requests for information should be addressed to:

ZondervanPublishingHouse
*Grand Rapids, Michigan 49530*

ISBN 0-310-67857-9

*Interior design by Sherri Hoffman*

*Printed in the United States of America*

06  /❖ VG/ 10 09 08 07

# FAITH LESSONS

## ON THE prophets & KINGS OF ISRAEL

### LEADER'S GUIDE

## Also Available from Ray Vander Laan

### Video and Group Resources

Faith Lessons on the Death and Resurrection of the Messiah
Faith Lessons on the Life and Ministry of the Messiah
Faith Lessons on the Promised Land

### Book and Audiocassette

Echoes of His Presence

# contents

NOTE TO LEADERS: The videos for this series were originally published under the title, *That the World May Know, Faith Lessons 6–10*. If you are using this guide with the original video series, you will not have the video, "Innocent Blood—Highlights," which forms the basis for Session 2. "Innocent Blood—Highlights" is merely a condensation of "Innocent Blood" that has been developed to provide a quick review of the previous session. You may choose to show a few minutes of the original video for the Session 2, or you may choose to provide participants with a short verbal review before beginning the session.

# introduction

Because God speaks to us through the Scriptures, studying them is a rewarding experience. The inspired human authors of the Bible, as well as those to whom the words were originally given, were primarily Jews living in the Near East. God's words and actions spoke to them with such power, clarity, and purpose that they wrote them down and carefully preserved them as an authoritative body of literature.

God's use of human servants in revealing Himself resulted in writings that clearly bear the stamp of time and place. The message of the Scriptures is, of course, eternal and unchanging—but the circumstances and conditions of the people of the Bible are unique to their times. Consequently, we most clearly understand God's truth when we know the cultural context within which He spoke and acted and the perception of the people with whom He communicated. This does not mean that God's revelation is unclear if we don't know the cultural context. Rather, by learning how to think and approach life as Abraham, Moses, Ruth, Esther, and Paul did, modern Christians will deepen their appreciation of God's Word. To fully apply the message of the Bible, we must enter the world of the Hebrews and familiarize ourselves with their culture.

That is the purpose of this study. The events and characters of the Bible are presented in their original settings. Although the videos offer the latest archaeological research, this series is not intended to be a definitive cultural and geographical study of the lands of the Bible. No original scientific discoveries are revealed here. The purpose of this study is to help us better understand God's revealed mission for our lives by enabling us to hear and see His words in their original context.

## understanding the world of the hebrews

More than 3,800 years ago, God spoke to His servant Abraham: "Go, walk through the length and breadth of the land, for I am giving it to you" (Genesis 13:17). From the outset, God's choice of a Hebrew nomad to begin His plan of salvation (that is still unfolding) was linked to the selection of a specific land where His redemptive work would begin. The nature of God's covenant relationship with His people demanded a place where their faith could be exercised and displayed to all nations so that the world would know of *Yahweh*, the true and faithful God. God showed the same care in preparing a land for His chosen people as He did in preparing a people to live in that land. For us to fully understand God's plan and purpose for His people, we must first understand the nature of the place He selected for them.

By New Testament times, the Jewish people had been removed from the Promised Land by the Babylonians due to Israel's failure to live obediently before God (Jeremiah 25:4–11). The exile lasted seventy years, but its impact upon God's people was astounding. New patterns of worship developed, and scribes and experts in God's law shaped the new commitment to be faithful to Him. The prophets predicted the appearance of a Messiah like King David who would revive the kingdom of the Hebrew people.

But the Promised Land was now home to many other groups of people whose religious practices, moral values, and lifestyles conflicted with those of the Jews. Living as God's witnesses took on added difficulty as Greek, Roman, and Samaritan worldviews mingled with that of the Israelites. The Promised Land was divided between kings and governors, usually under the authority of one foreign empire or another. But the mission of God's people did not change. They were still to live *so that the world would know that their God was the true God.* And the land continued to provide them opportunity to encounter the world that desperately needed to know this reality.

The Promised Land was the arena within which God's people were to serve Him faithfully as the world watched. The land God chose for His people was on the crossroads of the world. A major trade route, the Via Maris, ran through it. God intended for the Israelites to take control of the cities along this route and thereby exert influence on the nations around them. Through their righteous living, the Hebrews were to reveal the one true God, *Yahweh,* to the world. They failed to accomplish this mission, however, because of their unfaithfulness.

Western Christianity tends to spiritualize the concept of the Promised Land as it is presented in the Bible. Instead of seeing it as a crossroads from which to influence the world, modern Christians view it as a distant, heavenly city, a glorious "Canaan" toward which we are traveling as we ignore the world around us. We are focused on the destination, not the journey. We have unconsciously separated our walk with God from our responsibility to the world in which He has placed us. In one sense, our earthly experience is simply preparation for an eternity in the "promised land." Preoccupation with this idea, however, distorts the mission God has set for us.

Living by faith is not a vague, otherworldly experience; rather, it is being faithful to God right now, in the place and time in which He has put us. This truth is emphasized by God's choice of Canaan, a crossroads of the ancient world, as the Promised Land for the Israelites. God wants His people to be in the game, not on the bench. Our mission, as Christians today, is the same one He gave to the Israelites. We are to live obediently *within* the world so that through us *the world may know that our God is the one true God.*

# The Assumptions of Biblical Writers

Biblical writers assumed that their readers were familiar with Near Eastern geography. The geography of Canaan shaped the culture of the people living there. Their settlements began near sources of water and food. Climate and raw materials shaped their choice of occupation, dress, weapons, diet, and even artistic expression. As their cities grew, they interacted politically. Trade developed, and trade routes were established.

During New Testament times, the Promised Land was called Palestine or Judea. *Judea* (which means "Jewish") technically referred to the land that had been the nation of Judah. Because of the influence that the people of Judea had over the rest of the land, the land itself was called Judea. The Romans divided the land into several provinces, including Judea, Samaria, and Galilee (the three main divisions during Jesus' time); Gaulanitis, the Decapolis, and Perea (east of the Jordan River); and Idumaea (Edom) and Nabatea (in the south). These further divisions of Israel added to the rich historical and cultural background God prepared for the coming of Jesus and the beginning of His church.

Today the names *Israel* and *Palestine* are often used to designate the land God gave to Abraham. Both terms are politically charged. *Palestine* is used by the Arabs living in the central part of the country, while *Israel* is used by the Jews to indicate the State of Israel. In this study, *Israel* is used in the biblical sense. This choice does not indicate a political statement regarding the current struggle in the Middle East but instead is chosen to best reflect the biblical designation for the land.

Unfortunately, many Christians do not have even a basic geographical knowledge of the region. This series is designed to help solve that problem. We will be studying the people and events of the Bible in their geographical and historical contexts. Once we know the *who, what,* and *where* of a Bible story, we will be able to understand the *why.* By deepening our understanding of God's Word, we can strengthen our relationship with God.

The biblical writers also used a language that, like all languages, is bound by culture and time. Therefore, understanding the Scriptures involves more than knowing what the words mean. We need to also understand those words from the perspective of the people who used them.

The people whom God chose as His instruments—the people to whom He revealed Himself—were Hebrews living in the Near East. These people described their world and themselves in concrete terms. Their language was one of pictures, metaphors, and examples rather than ideas, definitions, and abstractions. Whereas we might describe God as omniscient or omnipresent (knowing everything and present everywhere), a Hebrew would have preferred to describe God by saying, "The Lord is my shepherd." Thus, the Bible is filled with concrete images from Hebrew culture: God is our Father, and we are His children; God is the potter, and we are the clay; Jesus is the Lamb killed on Passover; Heaven is an oasis in the desert; and hell is the city sewage dump; the Last Judgment will be in the Eastern Gate of the heavenly Jerusalem and will include sheep and goats.

These people had an Eastern mindset rather than a Western mindset. Eastern thought emphasizes the process of learning as much or more than the end result. Whereas Westerners tend to collect information to find the right answer, Hebrew thought stresses the process of discovery as well as the answer. Thus in the Leader's Guide we have included *suggested responses* to the questions. These are provided primarily to help the leader determine the area(s) on which the participants should focus in discovering the answer(s). These suggested responses are not intended to be the final answers or provide an exhaustive list of possible responses. So, the effective leader will allow the participants to process the information and will stress the learning value of that process.

# How to Use This Guide

This Leader's Guide is divided into six sessions approximately 50–55 minutes in length. Each session corresponds to a videotaped presentation by Ray Vander Laan.

For each session, *the leader* will need:

- Leader's Guide
- Bible
- Video player, monitor, stand, extension cord, etc.
- Videotape

*Note:* For some sessions, the leader may also want to use an overhead projector, chalk board, or marker board.

For each session, *the participant* will need:

- Participant's Guide
- Bible
- Pen or pencil

Directions to the leader are enclosed in the shaded boxes and are not meant to be spoken.

Each session is divided into six main parts: **Before You Lead**, **Introduction**, **Video Presentation**, **Group Discovery**, **Faith Lesson**, and **Closing Prayer**. A brief explanation of each part follows.

## 1. Before You Lead

### Synopsis

This material is presented for the leader's information. It summarizes the material presented in each of the videos.

### Key Points of This Lesson

Highlights the key points you'll want to emphasize.

### Session Outline

Provides an overview of the content and activities to be covered throughout the session.

### Materials

The materials listed above are critical for both the leader and each participant. Additional materials (optional) are listed when appropriate.

# 2. introduction

### Welcome

Welcomes participants to the session.

### What's to Come

A brief summary you may choose to use as you begin the session.

### Questions to Think About

Designed to help everyone begin thinking about the theme or topics that will be covered. A corresponding page is included in the Participant's Guide.

# 3. video presentation

This is the time during which you and the participants will watch the video and write down appropriate notes. Key themes have been indicated.

# 4. Group Discovery

In this section, you'll guide participants in thinking through materials and themes related to the video you've just seen. You may want to read the material word for word, or simply highlight key words and phrases. Feel free to amplify various points with your own material or illustrations.

The Leader's Guide includes a copy of the corresponding pages in the Participant's Guide. Space is also provided in which to write additional planning notes. Having the Participant's Guide pages in front of you allows you to view the pages the participants are seeing as you talk without having to hold two books at the same time. It also lets you know where the participants are in their book when someone asks you a question.

### Video Highlights

Use these questions and suggested responses with the entire group. This will guide participants in verbally responding to key points/themes covered in the video.

### Small Group Bible Discovery

At this time, if your group has more than seven participants you will break the group into small groups (three to five people) and assign each group a topic. (If you have more groups than topics, assign some topics to more than one group.) Participants will use their Bibles and write down suggested responses to the questions. At the end of this discovery time, participants will reassemble as a large group. As time allows, small group representatives can share key ideas their groups discussed.

Quite often supplementary material—called *Data File*, *Profile*, etc.—has been inserted near the topics. This material complements the themes but is not required reading to complete the session. Suggest that the participants read and study the supplementary material on their own.

## 5. faith Lesson

### Time for Reflection

At this time, participants will read selected Scripture passages on their own and think about questions that encourage them to apply what they've just discovered to their own lives.

### Action Points

At this time, you'll summarize key points (provided for you) with the entire group and encourage participants to act on what they have learned.

## 6. closing prayer

Close the session with the material or prayer provided.

### Before the First Session

- Watch the video session.
- Obtain the necessary Participant's Guides for all participants.
- Make sure you have the necessary equipment.

## Tips for Leading and promoting group Discussion

1. Allow group members to participate at their own comfort level. Everyone need not answer every question.
2. Ask questions with interest and warmth and then listen carefully to individual responses. Remember: it is important for participants to think through the questions and ideas presented. The *process* is more important than specific *answers*, which is why *suggested responses* are provided.
3. Be flexible. Reword questions if necessary. Choose to spend more time on a topic. Add or delete questions to accommodate the needs of your group members—and your time frame.
4. Suggest that participants, during the coming week, do the Small Group Bible Discovery topics that their individual small groups may not have had the opportunity to do.
5. Allow for (and expect) differences of opinion and experience.
6. Gently guide all participants into discussion. Do not allow any person(s) to monopolize discussion.
7. Should a heated discussion begin on a theological topic, suggest that the participants involved continue their discussion after the session is over.
8. Do not be afraid of silence. Allow people time to think—don't panic. Sometimes ten seconds of silence seems like an eternity. Remember, some of this material requires time to process—so allow people time to digest a question and *then* respond.

# Innocent Blood—Part I

## Before You Lead

Because of the length and powerful message of this video, it will require two sessions to adequately cover the material presented. Part one will involve viewing the entire video followed by times for discussion and personal reflection. Part two will include a condensed version of the video for review followed by times for Bible discovery, personal reflection, and action points.

### Synopsis

Tel Megiddo, where this session was filmed, was the greatest of the ancient cities of Israel. It was strategically located next to a crucial mountain pass overlooking the Plain of Jezreel. The Via Maris—the international trade route of the day—ran through this pass, so whoever controlled Megiddo also controlled the trade of the ancient world and exerted great influence on world culture. In fact, 1 Kings 9 reveals that Solomon gained much of his wealth because God gave him the power to control the Via Maris. Because of the importance of Megiddo's location, some scholars believe that more battles have been fought in the Jezreel Valley than in any other place in the world.

But Megiddo represents more than political control and economic and cultural influence. It also represents the battle for spiritual control—the battle between good and evil—that continues to this day and will culminate in the battle of *Har Megiddo,* or Armageddon.

Centuries before the Hebrew people settled in the Promised Land (from about 2950–2350 B.C.), Megiddo was a prominent "high place" where the Canaanite people worshiped their fertility god, Baal, and his supposed mistress, Asherah. When the ancient Israelites settled in the land, their beliefs and values clashed with those of the Canaanite residents. The worship of the Canaanite gods demonstrated a blatant disregard for human life and God's laws concerning human sexuality. Unfortunately, those ungodly attitudes and practices greatly shaped the culture and induced the Israelites to participate in Baal worship as well.

Over time, the worship of Baal became more and more a part of life for the Israelites. The gods of fertility, who were supposed to be responsible for providing rain for the lush crops of the Jezreel Valley, had an appeal that the Israelites' God, whom they viewed primarily as the God of the desert wilderness, did not have. The people drew further away from God, and eventually even the kings of Israel—especially King Ahab and his wife Jezebel (who had been a priestess of Baal in her homeland of Phoenicia)—encouraged Baal worship.

The rituals of Baal worship included sexual intercourse with temple prostitutes and the sacrifice of children in order to induce the gods to provide rain for the crops. Thus, as Ray Vander Laan points out, the Israelites sacrificed their children in order to ensure personal gain and success. These practices also perverted two of the most beautiful gifts God gave humankind: the gift of human life and the sexual relationship between a husband and wife within the bonds of marriage. Viewers will feel the horror of these abominable practices and will be challenged to consider the ways in which they also pervert God's gifts.

In this video, Ray Vander Laan emphasizes that the true significance of Megiddo is found in the spiritual battle for control of the hearts, minds, and souls of the people. That battle is represented by the high place at Megiddo, but it didn't end there. Christians today are also a part of the spiritual battle between good and evil that continues to take place throughout the world. So we must exert influence on the "Megiddos" of our world—the strategic places where culture can be influenced—whether they be Hollywood, Wall Street, Washington, D.C., or our families.

The battle in our culture between good and evil has great consequences. People who stand firm for God, who promote His principles in an increasingly pagan world, and who resist sinful and seductive influences are fighting a tough battle, a battle that will continue until the end of the world. Yet God's people can take heart. Jesus grew up in Nazareth, within sight of Megiddo, and lived there until He began His public ministry. How often He must have looked at Megiddo, knowing what had happened there, what it represented in His day, and what it would stand for in the future. In a sense, His work began at Armageddon and will one day end at Armageddon when His victory over evil is complete.

## Key Points of This Lesson

1. Located above the Valley of Jezreel, Megiddo stood guard over the Via Maris at a key mountain pass; whoever controlled the city controlled the trade route. Within sight of that city, terrible battles took place in the Plain of Jezreel. *Today, as in ancient Israel, great spiritual battles are taking place throughout the world between the people of God and the people of evil, between the values of God and the values of Satan. They are battles for the hearts, minds, and souls of people—and the consequences are great.*

2. *The Israelites were called to serve God, who loves innocence. But during King Ahab's reign, while they claimed to worship God, they also worshiped the evil gods of Canaan (especially Baal) and sacrificed their children for personal gain.* God strongly condemned their claim to honor Him while they engaged in such abominable practices.

   Today, we face similar choices. How easy it can be to honor God, on the one hand, and yet allow sinful patterns of thought and action to remain rooted in our lives. How easy it can be to sacrifice others in order to gain personal blessing and achieve "success."

3. *Megiddo also stands as a symbol of hope and promise.* It reminds us that the battle between good and evil is ultimately the battle for control of the world. Because of the redemptive work of Jesus Christ, those who engage in the battle against evil can take heart. For when the battle is finally over, Jesus Christ will be the victor. He will be crowned King of Kings!

### Session Outline (52 minutes)

I. **Introduction** (5 minutes)
Welcome
What's to Come
Questions to Think About

II. **Show Video "Innocent Blood"** (33 minutes)

III. **Group Discovery** (7 minutes)
Video Highlights

IV. **Faith Lesson** (5 minutes)
Time for Reflection

V. **Closing Prayer** (2 minutes)

## Materials

No additional materials are needed for this session. Simply view the video prior to leading the session so you are familiar with its main points.

# innocent blood—part 1

## introduction

**5** minutes

**Welcome**

> Assemble the participants together. Welcome them to session one of *Faith Lessons on the Prophets and Kings of Israel.*

**What's to Come**

Today our attention is drawn to the ancient city of Megiddo, which has played an important role in Israel's history and promises to play an important role in the future. Towering above the Plain of Jezreel and the Via Maris, the city was the defining point for economic and political control of the ancient world. The city also represents a defining point in the battle for spiritual control of the people.

In this video, the ongoing battle between good and evil—the battle for control of the hearts, souls, and minds of the people—will be powerfully demonstrated. We'll also see how important it is to participate in the spiritual battle between good and evil and to influence culture in strategic ways. Because of the length and nature of the material covered in this session, our format will be a bit different from that of subsequent sessions. We will take two sessions to complete the study of this video, focusing our attention on the video this week and on the Bible discovery next week. Let's begin with a few questions that will prepare our hearts and minds to receive the message of this video.

**Questions to Think About**

> *Participant's Guide page 13.*

> Ask each question and solicit a few responses from group members.

1. How do you think a historian 150 years from now would describe our culture's values and life priorities? How might that historian evaluate the current status of the battle between good and evil?

   *Suggested Responses:* These will vary. Encourage participants to identify the issues, beliefs, and practices in which the battle between good and evil is intense and readily evident as well as where it is more subtle. Issues regarding the value

**SESSION ONE**

# innocent blood—part 1

## questions to think about

1. How do you think a historian 150 years from now would describe our culture's values and life priorities? How might that historian evaluate the current status of the battle between good and evil?

2. Today, many of us really want to "succeed" in life and will sacrifice a great deal in order to achieve personal benefits. Yet innocent people around us can be harmed by our choices. Give a few examples of how striving for personal success or gain can harm other people. You may use your own experiences or the experiences of people you know as examples.

13

of human life—abortion, homelessness, and care of the elderly or infirm—would be examples.

✏ 2.  Today, many of us really want to "succeed" in life and will sacrifice a great deal in order to achieve personal benefits. Yet innocent people around us can be harmed by our choices. Give a few examples of how striving for personal success or gain can harm other people. You may use your own experiences or the experiences of people you know as examples.

*Suggested Responses:* These will vary, but may include men and women who put more effort into their careers than their marriages; children who don't receive adequate attention from their parents because of their parents' devotion to other pursuits; people who are so consumed by their own interests that they cannot see the needs of others; people who "use" other people in order to promote themselves; etc.

Let's keep these ideas in mind as we view the video.

## IT'S WORTH OBSERVING . . .

### The Struggle for Our Hearts and Minds

When the Israelites—nomad Hebrews—entered Canaan, they discovered a lush land of farmers, not shepherds. The Canaanites attributed this fertility to their god, Baal. Because people of that time thought of their gods in terms of a specific place, the Israelites wondered if their God, whom they perceived to be the God of the desert wilderness, was still their God in the vastly different land of Canaan. The Israelites were wondering, *Can Yahweh, who led us out of Egypt and through the wilderness, also provide fertile crops in Canaan, or do we have to honor Baal? Or do we honor both?*

An intense spiritual battle began for the hearts and minds of God's people. Over and over again in the Old Testament, we read about the Israelites' attraction to and worship of Canaanite gods, God's disciplinary response, the people's repentance, and God's merciful forgiveness. Then the cycle would repeat itself.

By the time of Ahab and Jezebel, the fertility cults seem to have had the official sanction of Israel's leaders. Ahab, with his wife's encouragement, built a temple to Baal in his capital, Samaria. Yet, prophets like Elijah (whose name means "Yahweh is God"), Hosea, Isaiah, and Jeremiah thundered that Yahweh alone deserved the people's allegiance. It took the destruction of Israel by the Assyrians and the Babylonian captivity of Judah to convince the Israelites that there is only one omnipotent God.

The struggle to be totally committed to God is of vital importance to us today, too. We don't think of ourselves as idol worshipers, yet we struggle to serve God in every part of our lives. It is easy (and seductive) to honor self, possessions, fun, relationships, fame, money, and many other gods.

**SESSION ONE**

# innocent blood—part 1

## questions to think about

1. How do you think a historian 150 years from now would
   describe our culture's values and life priorities? How might
   that historian evaluate the current status of the battle
   between good and evil?

2. Today, many of us really want to "succeed" in life and will
   sacrifice a great deal in order to achieve personal benefits.
   Yet innocent people around us can be harmed by our
   choices. Give a few examples of how striving for personal
   success or gain can harm other people. You may use your
   own experiences or the experiences of people you know
   as examples.

13

14                Faith Lessons on the Prophets and Kings of Israel

### IT'S WORTH OBSERVING . . .

**The Struggle for Our Hearts and Minds**

When the Israelites—nomad Hebrews—entered Canaan, they discovered a lush land of farmers, not shepherds. The Canaanites attributed this fertility to their god, Baal. Because people of that time thought of their gods in terms of a specific place, the Israelites wondered if their God, whom they perceived to be the God of the desert wilderness, was still their God in the vastly different land of Canaan. The Israelites were wondering, *Can Yahweh, who led us out of Egypt and through the wilderness also provide fertile crops in Canaan, or do we have to honor Baal? Or do we honor both?*

An intense spiritual battle began for the hearts and minds of God's people. Over and over again in the Old Testament, we read about the Israelites' attraction to and worship of Canaanite gods, God's disciplinary response, the people's repentance, and God's merciful forgiveness. Then the cycle would repeat itself.

By the time of Ahab and Jezebel, the fertility cults seem to have had the official sanction of Israel's leaders. Ahab, with his wife's encouragement, built a temple to Baal in his capital, Samaria. Yet, prophets like Elijah (whose name means "Yahweh is God"), Hosea, Isaiah, and Jeremiah thundered that Yahweh alone deserved the people's allegiance. It took the destruction of Israel by the Assyrians and the Babylonian captivity of Judah to convince the Israelites that there is only one omnipotent God.

The struggle to be totally committed to God is of vital importance to us today, too. We don't think of ourselves as idol worshipers, yet we struggle to serve God in every part of our lives. It is easy (and seductive) to honor self, possessions, fun, relationships, fame, money, and many other gods.

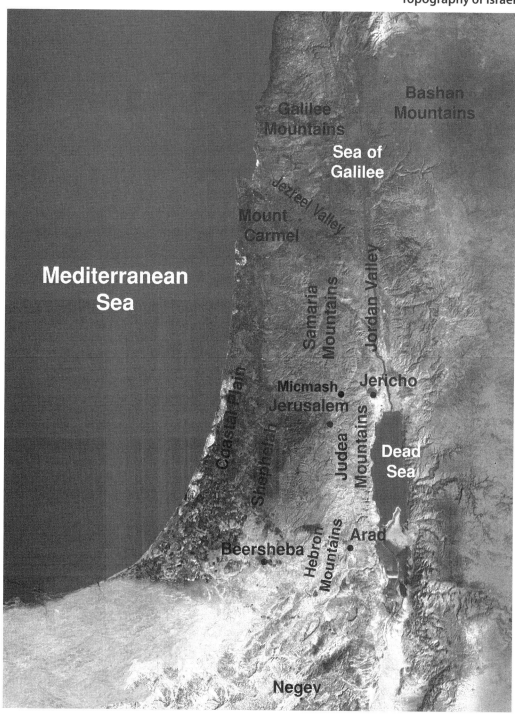

Topography of Israel

PLANNING NOTES:

# video presentation

*Participant's Guide page 16.*

On page 16 of your Participant's Guide, you will find a space in which to take notes on key points as we watch this video.

### Leader's Video Observations

Megiddo

The Place

The Battleground for Control of the World

Baal Worship

The Battle for Good and Evil in Our Culture

## video notes

**Megiddo**

The Place

The Battleground for Control of the World

**Baal Worship**

**The Battle for Good and Evil in Our Culture**

# Group Discovery

**Video Highlights (7 minutes)**

> Here you'll ask one or more of the following questions that directly relate to the video the participants have just seen.

1. Which images from the video made the most powerful impression on you? Why?

   *Suggested Responses:* These will vary. Allow participants to share their impressions.

2. What thoughts are foremost in your mind as a result of seeing this video?

   *Suggested Responses:* These will vary. Allow participants to share their thoughts.

3. What did the Israelites and Canaanites hope to gain by sacrificing their children to Baal?

   *Suggested Response:* They wanted what they believed Baal would provide: good crop yields that would bring personal success and material gain.

4. Do you agree that there are some remarkable similarities between our culture today and the culture of the Israelites when they worshiped both Baal and God? What similarities can you identify?

   *Suggested Responses:* These will vary but may include a diminished view of the value of life; public and unashamed perversion of God's gift of sexuality; a willingness to do (almost) anything to ensure one's personal success and comfort; a desire for spirituality accompanied by confusion about God's true identity and role in our lives; etc.

5. What was God's response to the Israelites' worship of Baal, particularly the sacrifice of infants?

   *Suggested Responses:* God condemned it; He detested it; He even considered their worship of Him to be a desecration of His temple because of it; He was so appalled by it that He said the idea of it never even entered His mind; He determined to put an end to it by destroying the culture; etc.

6. What would God's response to child sacrifice be today?

   *Suggested Responses:* It would not be any different because He will not tolerate the shedding of innocent blood.

> As soon as participants have spent seven minutes discussing the above questions, direct the entire group's attention to the next section.

## video highlights

1. Which images from the video made the most powerful impression on you? Why?

2. What thoughts are foremost in your mind as a result of seeing this video?

3. What did the Israelites and Canaanites hope to gain by sacrificing their children to Baal?

4. Do you agree that there are some remarkable similarities between our culture today and the culture of the Israelites when they worshiped both Baal and God? What similarities can you identify?

5. What was God's response to the Israelites' worship of Baal, particularly the sacrifice of infants?

6. What would God's response to child sacrifice be today?

## DATA FILE

### The Gods of Canaan

#### *Baal*

The earliest deity recognized by people of the ancient Near East was the creator-god, El. His mistress, the fertility goddess Asherah, supposedly gave birth to many gods, including a powerful one named Baal ("Lord"). There appears to have been only one Baal, who was manifested in lesser Baals at different times and places. Over the years, Baal became the dominant deity, and the worship of El faded away.

Baal supposedly won his dominance by defeating other deities, including the god of the sea, god of storms (also of rain, thunder, and lightning), and god of death. His victory over death was thought to be repeated each year when he returned from the land of death (the underworld) and brought rain to renew the earth's fertility.

Hebrew culture viewed the sea as evil and destructive, so Baal's promise to prevent storms and control the sea, as well as his seeming ability to produce abundant harvests, made him attractive to the Israelites. It's difficult to understand why Yahweh's people failed to see that He alone had power over these things. Possibly their desert origins led them to question God's sovereignty over fertile land. Maybe, however, the sinful pagan practices attracted them to Baal.

Baal is portrayed as a man who had the head and horns of a bull, an image similar to that in biblical accounts. His right hand (and sometimes both hands) was raised, and he held a lightning bolt that signified destruction and fertility. Baal was sometimes seated on a throne, possibly to show that he was the king or lord of the gods.

Baal worshipers appeased him by offering sacrifices, usually sheep and bulls (1 Kings 18:26). Some scholars believe that the Canaanites also sacrificed pigs and that God prohibited His people from eating pork in part to prevent this horrible cult from being established among them. (See Isaiah 65:1–5 for an example of Israel's participation in the Canaanites' pagan practices.)

(continued on page 28)

**Baal Sacrifice Altar**

## DATA FILE

### The Gods of Canaan

#### Baal

The earliest deity recognized by people of the ancient Near East was the creator-god, El. His mistress, the fertility goddess Asherah, supposedly gave birth to many gods, including a powerful one named Baal ("Lord"). There appears to have been only one Baal, who was manifested in lesser Baals at different times and places. Over the years, Baal became the dominant deity, and the worship of El faded away.

Baal supposedly won his dominance by defeating other deities, including the god of the sea, god of storms (also of rain, thunder, and lightning), and god of death. His victory over death was thought to be repeated each year when he returned from the land of death (the underworld) and brought rain to renew the earth's fertility.

Hebrew culture viewed the sea as evil and destructive, so Baal's promise to prevent storms and control the sea, as well as his seeming ability to produce abundant harvests, made him attractive to the Israelites. It's difficult to understand why Yahweh's people failed to see that He alone had power over these things. Possibly their desert origins led them to question God's sovereignty over fertile land. Maybe, however, the sinful pagan practices attracted them to Baal.

Baal is portrayed as a man who had the head and horns of a bull, an image similar to that in biblical accounts. His right hand (and sometimes both hands) was raised, and he held a lightning bolt that signified destruction and fertility. Baal was sometimes seated on a throne, possibly to show that he was the king or lord of the gods.

Baal worshipers appeased him by offering sacrifices, usually sheep and bulls (1 Kings 18:26). Some scholars believe that the Canaanites also sacrificed pigs and that God prohibited His people from eating pork in part to prevent this horrible cult from being established among them. (See Isaiah 65:1–5 for an example of Israel's participation in the Canaanites' pagan practices.)

(continued on page 20)

---

**Baal Sacrifice Altar**

(continued from page 19)

During times of crisis, Baal's followers sacrificed their children, apparently the firstborn of the community, in order to gain personal prosperity. The Bible calls this practice "detestable" (Deuteronomy 12:31; 18:9–10). God specifically appointed the tribe of Levi to be His special servants, in place of the firstborn of the Israelites, so they had no excuse for offering their children (Numbers 3:11–13). God hated child sacrifice, especially among those who were called to be His people.

#### Asherah

Asherah, in various forms and with varying names, was honored as the fertility goddess (Judges 3:7). The Bible does not actually describe her, but archaeologists have discovered figurines believed to be representations of her. She is portrayed as a nude female, sometimes pregnant, with exaggerated breasts that she holds out apparently as symbols of her fertility. The Bible indicates that she was worshiped near trees and poles, called Asherah poles (Deuteronomy 7:5; 12:2–3; 2 Kings 16:4; 17:10; Jeremiah 3:6,13; Ezekiel 6:13).

(continued from page 26)

During times of crisis, Baal's followers sacrificed their children, apparently the firstborn of the community, in order to gain personal prosperity. The Bible calls this practice "detestable" (Deuteronomy 12:31; 18:9–10). God specifically appointed the tribe of Levi to be His special servants, in place of the firstborn of the Israelites, so they had no excuse for offering their children (Numbers 3:11–13). God hated child sacrifice, especially among those who were called to be His people.

### Asherah

Asherah, in various forms and with varying names, was honored as the fertility goddess (Judges 3:7). The Bible does not actually describe her, but archaeologists have discovered figurines believed to be representations of her. She is portrayed as a nude female, sometimes pregnant, with exaggerated breasts that she holds out apparently as symbols of her fertility. The Bible indicates that she was worshiped near trees and poles, called Asherah poles (Deuteronomy 7:5; 12:2–3; 2 Kings 16:4; 17:10; Jeremiah 3:6,13; Ezekiel 6:13).

**The Goddess Asherah**

Asherah was worshiped in various ways, including ritual sex. Although she was believed to be Baal's mother, she was also his mistress. Pagans practiced "sympathetic magic"—that is, they believed they could influence the gods' actions by performing the behavior they wished the gods to demonstrate. Believing that the sexual union of Baal and Asherah produced fertility, their worshipers engaged in immoral sex to cause the gods to join together and thereby ensure good harvests. This practice became the basis for religious prostitution (1 Kings 14:23–24). The priest or a male community member represented Baal. The priestess or a female community member represented Asherah. Thus God's incredible gift of sexuality within the bonds of marriage was perverted and became obscene public prostitution. No wonder God's anger burned against His people and their leaders.

**Baal Sacrifice Altar**

(continued from page 19)

During times of crisis, Baal's followers sacrificed their children, apparently the firstborn of the community, in order to gain personal prosperity. The Bible calls this practice "detestable" (Deuteronomy 12:31; 18:9–10). God specifically appointed the tribe of Levi to be His special servants, in place of the firstborn of the Israelites, so they had no excuse for offering their children (Numbers 3:11–13). God hated child sacrifice, especially among those who were called to be His people.

*Asherah*

Asherah, in various forms and with varying names, was honored as the fertility goddess (Judges 3:7). The Bible does not actually describe her, but archaeologists have discovered figurines believed to be representations of her. She is portrayed as a nude female, sometimes pregnant, with exaggerated breasts that she holds out apparently as symbols of her fertility. The Bible indicates that she was worshiped near trees and poles, called Asherah poles (Deuteronomy 7:5; 12:2–3; 2 Kings 16:4; 17:10; Jeremiah 3:6,13; Ezekiel 6:13).

**The Goddess Asherah**

Asherah was worshiped in various ways, including ritual sex. Although she was believed to be Baal's mother, she was also his mistress. Pagans practiced "sympathetic magic"—that is, they believed they could influence the gods' actions by performing the behavior they wished the gods to demonstrate. Believing that the sexual union of Baal and Asherah produced fertility, their worshipers engaged in immoral sex to cause the gods to join together and thereby ensure good harvests. This practice became the basis for religious prostitution (1 Kings 14:23–24). The priest or a male community member represented Baal. The priestess or a female community member represented Asherah. Thus God's incredible gift of sexuality within the bonds of marriage was perverted and became obscene public prostitution. No wonder God's anger burned against His people and their leaders.

# faith Lesson

## Time for Reflection (5 minutes)

This video has certainly given us a great deal to think about. Let's take some time for each of us to begin processing what we've seen today. On page 22 of your Participant's Guide, you'll find a passage of Scripture. Read this passage silently and then consider some of the questions that follow.

Please do not talk during this time. It's a time when we all can reflect on how the message of this video applies to our lives.

> *The Scripture passage and questions are reproduced in their entirety in the Participant's Guide on pages 22-23.*

This is the word that came to Jeremiah from the LORD: "Stand at the gate of the LORD's house and there proclaim this message: 'Hear the word of the LORD, all you people of Judah who come through these gates to worship the LORD. This is what the LORD Almighty, the God of Israel, says: Reform your ways and your actions, and I will let you live in this place. Do not trust in deceptive words and say, "This is the temple of the LORD, the temple of the LORD, the temple of the LORD!" If you really change your ways and your actions and deal with each other justly, if you do not oppress the alien, the fatherless or the widow and do not shed innocent blood in this place, and if you do not follow other gods to your own harm, then I will let you live in this place, in the land I gave your forefathers for ever and ever. But look, you are trusting in deceptive words that are worthless. 'Will you steal and murder, commit adultery and perjury, burn incense to Baal and follow other gods you have not known, and then come and stand before me in this house, which bears my Name, and say, "We are safe"—safe to do all these detestable things?'"

JEREMIAH 7:1–10

1. During King Ahab's time, the Israelites were willing to sacrifice their children in a vain effort to influence Baal to give them good crop yields. What might you be sacrificing today in order to gain personal security and success? What do you want so badly that you are willing to sacrifice almost anything to obtain it?

2. It's easy to be critical of how the Israelites worshiped God and yet sacrificed their children to Baal, but what sinful patterns of belief or behavior are you holding onto? In what ways might you be mixing righteousness with evil?

3. In what way(s) do the lessons the Israelites learned concerning sin's attractiveness apply to your life and your culture?

4. How would God have you respond to the sins of your culture and your sins?

## faith Lesson

**Time for Reflection**

Read the following passage of Scripture and take the next few minutes to reflect on how the message of this video applies to your life.

This is the word that came to Jeremiah from the LORD: "Stand at the gate of the LORD's house and there proclaim this message: 'Hear the word of the LORD, all you people of Judah who come through these gates to worship the LORD. This is what the LORD Almighty, the God of Israel, says: Reform your ways and your actions, and I will let you live in this place. Do not trust in deceptive words and say, "This is the temple of the LORD, the temple of the LORD, the temple of the LORD!" If you really change your ways and your actions and deal with each other justly, if you do not oppress the alien, the fatherless or the widow and do not shed innocent blood in this place, and if you do not follow other gods to your own harm, then I will let you live in this place, in the land I gave your forefathers for ever and ever. But look, you are trusting in deceptive words that are worthless. Will you steal and murder, commit adultery and perjury, burn incense to Baal and follow other gods you have not known, and then come and stand before me in this house, which bears my Name, and say, "We are safe"—safe to do all these detestable things?'"

JEREMIAH 7:1–10

1. During King Ahab's time, the Israelites were willing to sacrifice their children in a vain effort to influence Baal to give them good crop yields. What might you be sacrificing today in order to gain personal security and success? What do you want so badly that you are willing to sacrifice almost anything to obtain it?

2. It's easy to be critical of how the Israelites worshiped God and yet sacrificed their children to Baal, but what sinful patterns of belief or behavior are you holding onto? In what ways might you be mixing righteousness with evil?

3. In what way(s) do the lessons the Israelites learned concerning sin's attractiveness apply to your life and your culture?

4. How would God have you respond to the sins of your culture and your sins?

**THE ISSUES REMAIN THE SAME**

Canaan's fertility cults and practices have parallels in our day. In spite of our pride in development and technology, Western culture demonstrates a growing disregard for the sacredness of human life and regularly terminates it for personal convenience. Sexuality, too, has become the goddess of much of our society—notice how it is promoted in the arts, media, music, and advertising—as if genuine success in life depends on sexual prowess and a beautiful appearance.

Human beings haven't changed much in 3,000 years. God certainly hasn't changed. He still detests the devaluation of human life, whether that occurs through abortion, oppression, ethnic cleansing, or euthanasia. He also abhors the ways in which we have perverted our sexuality.

As Christians, we are called to obey God's laws concerning sexuality and the sacredness of human life. We are also called to prophetically address the sinfulness of our culture and demonstrate by example that obeying God's laws leads to true fulfillment.

# closing prayer

**2** minutes

Now it's time to wrap up our session.

Give participants a moment to transition from their thoughtfulness to giving you their full attention.

I hope that this session has challenged you, as it has me, to consider ways in which we are not being pure in our lives and may be sacrificing the wrong things in order to gain personal success. Let's close in prayer now.

*Dear God, You know the battles each of us is involved in today, battles that truly make a difference to our families, communities, and even our country. Make us aware of sins we harbor while we outwardly worship You. We want to draw closer to You and not worship the gods of our culture—the fame, money, beliefs, and relationships—that so seductively seek to attract us. Thank You that You have defeated evil and that You will return again to claim Your victory. Until that time, give us the strength to resist the gods of this world and give us the courage to influence the Megiddos of our culture so that they will reflect more of You and Your values. In Jesus' name we pray, amen.*

### THE ISSUES REMAIN THE SAME

Canaan's fertility cults and practices have parallels in our day. In spite of our pride in development and technology, Western culture demonstrates a growing disregard for the sacredness of human life and regularly terminates it for personal convenience. Sexuality, too, has become the goddess of much of our society—notice how it is promoted in the arts, media, music, and advertising—as if genuine success in life depends on sexual prowess and a beautiful appearance.

Human beings haven't changed much in 3,000 years. God certainly hasn't changed. He still detests the devaluation of human life, whether that occurs through abortion, oppression, ethnic cleansing, or euthanasia. He also abhors the ways in which we have perverted our sexuality.

As Christians, we are called to obey God's laws concerning sexuality and the sacredness of human life. We are also called to prophetically address the sinfulness of our culture and demonstrate by example that obeying God's laws leads to true fulfillment.

**The Valley of Jezreel Viewed Across the Altar at Megiddo**

**DID YOU KNOW?**

The word *Armageddon*, the final battle described in Revelation 16:16, is derived from the Hebrew word *Har* (that means a "hill," "mound," or "mount") and *Megiddon* (that means "Megiddo"). By choosing Megiddo to be the symbol of the end-times battle, the writer of Revelation revealed that the final battle of Armageddon will determine who will ultimately control the world. (Note: Some Christians believe the reference to Armageddon is symbolic; others believe that a literal battle for world domination will take place.)

**The Valley of Jezreel Viewed Across the Altar at Megiddo**

24          Faith Lessons on the Prophets and Kings of Israel

### THE ISSUES REMAIN THE SAME

Canaan's fertility cults and practices have parallels in our day. In spite of our pride in development and technology, Western culture demonstrates a growing disregard for the sacredness of human life and regularly terminates it for personal convenience. Sexuality, too, has become the goddess of much of our society—notice how it is promoted in the arts, media, music, and advertising—as if genuine success in life depends on sexual prowess and a beautiful appearance.

Human beings haven't changed much in 3,000 years. God certainly hasn't changed. He still detests the devaluation of human life, whether that occurs through abortion, oppression, ethnic cleansing, or euthanasia. He also abhors the ways in which we have perverted our sexuality.

As Christians, we are called to obey God's laws concerning sexuality and the sacredness of human life. We are also called to prophetically address the sinfulness of our culture and demonstrate by example that obeying God's laws leads to true fulfillment.

**The Valley of Jezreel Viewed Across the Altar at Megiddo**

---

### DID YOU KNOW?

The word *Armageddon*, the final battle described in Revelation 16:16, is derived from the Hebrew word *Har* (that means a "hill," "mound," or "mount") and *Megiddon* (that means "Megiddo"). By choosing Megiddo to be the symbol of the end-times battle, the writer of Revelation revealed that the final battle of Armageddon will determine who will ultimately control the world. (Note: Some Christians believe the reference to Armageddon is symbolic; others believe that a literal battle for world domination will take place.)

# ınnocent вlood—paɾt 2

## вefoɾe you leαd

This session completes the study begun in session one. The video for session two features highlights from the Innocent Blood video viewed during the previous session. It will serve as a review for participants who saw the video for session one and will provide participants who missed that session with sufficient background to fully participate in this session.

### Synopsis

See session one.

### Key Points of This Lesson

1. Located above the Valley of Jezreel, Megiddo stood guard over the Via Maris at a key mountain pass; whoever controlled the city controlled the trade route. Within sight of that city, terrible battles took place in the Plain of Jezreel. *Today, as in ancient Israel, great spiritual battles are taking place throughout the world between the people of God and the people of evil, between the values of God and the values of Satan. They are battles for the hearts, minds, and souls of people—and the consequences are great.*

2. *The Israelites were called to serve God, who loves innocence. But during King Ahab's reign, while they claimed to worship God, they also worshiped the evil gods of Canaan (especially Baal) and sacrificed their children for personal gain. God strongly condemned their claim to honor Him while they engaged in such abominable practices.*

   Today, we face similar choices. How easy it can be to honor God, on the one hand, and yet allow sinful patterns of thought and action to remain rooted in our lives. How easy it can be to sacrifice others in order to gain personal blessing and achieve "success."

3. *Megiddo also stands as a symbol of hope and promise. It reminds us that the battle between good and evil is ultimately the battle for control of the world. Because of the redemptive work of Jesus Christ, those who engage in the battle against evil can take heart. For when the battle is finally over, Jesus Christ will be the victor. He will be crowned King of Kings!*

### Session Outline (53 minutes)

**I. Introduction** (5 minutes)

Welcome

What's to Come

Questions to Think About

**II. Show Review Video "Innocent Blood Highlights"** (17 minutes)

**III. Group Discovery** (20 minutes)

Video Highlights

Small Group Bible Discovery

**IV. Faith Lesson** (9 minutes)

Time for Reflection

Action Points

**V. Closing Prayer** (2 minutes)

## Materials

No additional materials are needed for this session. Simply view the video prior to leading the session so you are familiar with its main points.

# innocent Blood—part 2

## introduction

**5** minutes    **Welcome**

> Assemble the participants together. Welcome them to session two of *Faith Lessons on the Prophets and Kings of Israel.*

### What's to Come

We will once again focus our attention on the ancient city of Megiddo, which has played an important role in Israel's history and promises to play an important role in the future.

In ancient times, Megiddo towered above the Plain of Jezreel and the Via Maris. Because of its location, the city was a strategic point for economic and political control of the ancient world. It was a highly visible place where God's people had the potential to exert His influence on world culture and actively participate in the ongoing battle between good and evil. Since ancient times—and even until the end of the world—Megiddo stands as a symbol of the spiritual battleground where the battle to control the hearts, souls, and minds of the world's people is fought. Today we will consider our role in influencing the Megiddos of our day. Let's begin by asking ourselves a few questions.

### Questions to Think About

> *Participant's Guide page 26.*

> Ask each question and solicit a few responses from group members.

1. The video we saw during our last session carried a powerful message. Would anyone like to share some thoughts that have stayed in your mind or influenced your life since our last session together?

   *Suggested Responses:* Allow participants to share how the previous video affected them. If they are slow to respond, share how it impacted your life.

2. Name some people whom you think have stepped into strategic places and influenced your culture for God. What enabled them to have an influence, perhaps where other people had failed? What motivated them? What commitment did they make to the task? What personal price did they pay?

**SESSION TWO**

# innocent blood—part 2

## questions to think about

1. The video we saw during our last session carried a powerful message. Would anyone like to share some thoughts that have stayed in your mind or influenced your life since our last session together?

2. Name some people whom you think have stepped into strategic places and influenced your culture for God. What enabled them to have an influence, perhaps where other people had failed? What motivated them? What commitment did they make to the task? What personal price did they pay?

26

*Suggested Responses:* Allow participants to explore the reality of what is required to conquer a Megiddo and use it as a point from which to influence the world for God.

Let's keep these thoughts in mind as we view the video.

# video presentation

17 minutes

*Participant's Guide page 27.*

On page 27 of your Participant's Guide, you will find a space in which to take notes on key points as we watch this video.

## Leader's Video Observations

Tel Megiddo—Strategic Point for World Control

Baal Versus God—The Battle for Spiritual Control

The Battle in Our Culture

# innocent blood—part 2

## questions to think about

1. The video we saw during our last session carried a power-ful message. Would anyone like to share some thoughts that have stayed in your mind or influenced your life since our last session together?

2. Name some people whom you think have stepped into strategic places and influenced your culture for God. What enabled them to have an influence, perhaps where other people had failed? What motivated them? What commit-ment did they make to the task? What personal price did they pay?

## video notes

**Tel Megiddo—Strategic Point for World Control**

**Baal Versus God—The Battle for Spiritual Control**

**The Battle in Our Culture**

# group Discovery

**2O** minutes

If your group has seven or more members, use the **Video Highlights** with the entire group (5 minutes), then break into small groups of three to five to discuss the **Small Group Bible Discovery** (10 minutes). Then reassemble the group to discuss the key points discovered (5 minutes).

If your group has fewer than seven members, begin with the **Video Highlights** (5 minutes), then do one or more of the topics found in the **Small Group Bible Discovery** as a group (10 minutes). Finally, spend five minutes at the end discussing points that had an impact on participants.

### Video Highlights (5 minutes)

Here you'll ask one or more of the following questions that directly relate to the video the participants have just seen.

1. Look at the maps of Israel on page 28 and in the Data File on page 31 of your Participant's Guide. As you study the political and geographic features of this map, why do you think God chose Israel to be the land in which His plan of salvation would unfold?

**The Middle Eastern World**

*Suggested Response:* God wanted to establish His people in a place where they could influence world culture by being a high-profile testimony to the world that He was God. Note: Make sure participants realize that Israel was at the crossroads of ancient civilization. Because of the forbidding Arabian Desert to the east, the only trade and military route between Mesopotamia and Egypt was the corridor of Israel.

# video нighlights

1.  Look at the maps of Israel on page 28 and in the Data File on page 31 of your Participant's Guide. As you study the political and geographic features of this map, why do you think God chose Israel to be the land in which His plan of salvation would unfold?

2.  Why was Megiddo such an important city during biblical times?

**The Valley of Jezreel**

---

**The Middle Eastern World**

2.  Why was Megiddo such an important city during biblical times?

    *Suggested Response:* It was located by a strategic mountain pass through which the Via Maris—the international trade route used by important ancient civilizations—passed. Whoever controlled Megiddo thereby controlled the Via Maris.

3.  Why do you think Ray Vander Laan emphasized the need for Christians to occupy the "Megiddos" in our culture—the important places such as Hollywood, Wall Street, and our families—that greatly influence our culture's value system?

    *Suggested Response:* By influencing such "Megiddos," we can help to shape our culture's values.

4.  Do you agree with Ray Vander Laan that the family may be the most significant "Megiddo" of today? Why or why not?

    *Suggested Responses:* These will vary. Encourage participants to seriously consider the role the family plays in the shaping of culture.

**The Valley of Jezreel**

## video Highlights

1. Look at the maps of Israel on page 28 and in the Data File on page 31 of your Participant's Guide. As you study the political and geographic features of this map, why do you think God chose Israel to be the land in which His plan of salvation would unfold?

2. Why was Megiddo such an important city during biblical times?

**The Valley of Jezreel**

---

3. Why do you think Ray Vander Laan emphasized the need for Christians to occupy the "Megiddos" in our culture—the important places such as Hollywood, Wall Street, and our families—that greatly influence our culture's value system?

4. Do you agree with Ray Vander Laan that the family may be the most significant "Megiddo" of today? Why or why not?

### DATA FILE

**The Via Maris—Lifeline of Civilizations**

*Why It Was Vital*

The rugged mountain ranges of Samaria, Judea, and Hebron cut through the middle of Israel, making east-west travel difficult. And the forbidding Arabian Desert to the east added to the transportation difficulties. Yet Egypt, Babylon, Assyria, and other civilizations required the exchange of vital goods. Thus, whoever controlled the road between these empires dominated international trade and exerted great influence upon other cultures.

*Its Location*

The road entered the Great Rift Valley from the east, near Hazor, and continued to the Sea of Galilee. Then it turned southwest into the Valley of Jezreel and cut through the ridge of Mount Carmel to reach the coastal plain. Only one of three passes through the Mount Carmel ridge provided relatively easy travel: the Iron Wadi, which was guarded by Megiddo, the most significant city in Canaan. Once past Mount Carmel, the road continued along the coast toward Egypt. The main route was several miles

## DATA FILE

### The Via Maris—Lifeline of Civilizations

#### Why It Was Vital

The rugged mountain ranges of Samaria, Judea, and Hebron cut through the middle of Israel, making east-west travel difficult. And the forbidding Arabian Desert to the east added to the transportation difficulties. Yet Egypt, Babylon, Assyria, and other civilizations required the exchange of vital goods. Thus, whoever controlled the road between these empires dominated international trade and exerted great influence upon other cultures.

#### Its Location

The road entered the Great Rift Valley from the east, near Hazor, and continued to the Sea of Galilee. Then it turned southwest into the Valley of Jezreel and cut through the ridge of Mount Carmel to reach the coastal plain. Only one of three passes through the Mount Carmel ridge provided relatively easy travel: the Iron Wadi, which was guarded by Megiddo, the most significant city in Canaan. Once past Mount Carmel, the road continued along the coast toward Egypt. The main route was several miles inland, which enabled travelers to avoid the swamplands caused by runoff from the Judea mountains that was trapped by coastal sand dunes.

#### Its Control Points

At Gezer, Hazor, and Megiddo, the Via Maris could be controlled easily. Gezer stood where the road passed between swamplands and mountains. Hazor and Megiddo stood where the road entered mountain passes. Megiddo guarded the most narrow pass.

#### Why Israel Lost Out

Because they were so afraid of the Philistines and the Canaanites, the Israelites stayed mainly in the mountains or in the Shephelah—the foothills between the mountains and the coastal plain. The Israelites rarely controlled the key cities along the Via Maris, so they never exerted the degree of influence upon world culture that God intended them to have.

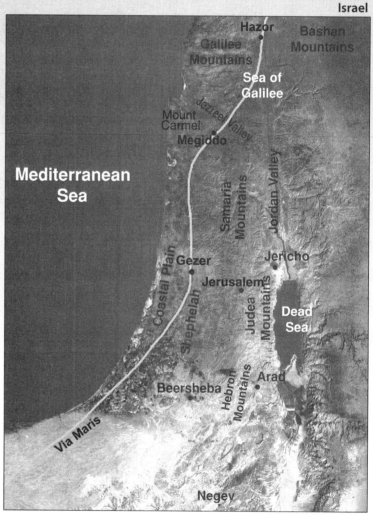

30          Faith Lessons on the Prophets and Kings of Israel

3. Why do you think Ray Vander Laan emphasized the need for Christians to occupy the "Megiddos" in our culture—the important places such as Hollywood, Wall Street, and our families—that greatly influence our culture's value system?

4. Do you agree with Ray Vander Laan that the family may be the most significant "Megiddo" of today? Why or why not?

### DATA FILE

**The Via Maris—Lifeline of Civilizations**

#### *Why It Was Vital*

The rugged mountain ranges of Samaria, Judea, and Hebron cut through the middle of Israel, making east-west travel difficult. And the forbidding Arabian Desert to the east added to the transportation difficulties. Yet Egypt, Babylon, Assyria, and other civilizations required the exchange of vital goods. Thus, whoever controlled the road between these empires dominated international trade and exerted great influence upon other cultures.

#### *Its Location*

The road entered the Great Rift Valley from the east, near Hazor, and continued to the Sea of Galilee. Then it turned southwest into the Valley of Jezreel and cut through the ridge of Mount Carmel to reach the coastal plain. Only one of three passes through the Mount Carmel ridge provided relatively easy travel: the Iron Wadi, which was guarded by Megiddo, the most significant city in Canaan. Once past Mount Carmel, the road continued along the coast toward Egypt. The main route was several miles

Session Two: Innocent Blood—Part 2                          31

inland, which enabled travelers to avoid the swamplands caused by runoff from the Judea mountains that was trapped by coastal sand dunes.

#### *Its Control Points*

At Gezer, Hazor, and Megiddo, the Via Maris could be controlled easily. Gezer stood where the road passed between swamplands and mountains. Hazor and Megiddo stood where the road entered mountain passes. Megiddo guarded the most narrow pass.

#### *Why Israel Lost Out*

Because they were so afraid of the Philistines and the Canaanites, the Israelites stayed mainly in the mountains or in the Shephelah—the foothills between the mountains and the coastal plain. The Israelites rarely controlled the key cities along the Via Maris, so they never exerted the degree of influence upon world culture that God intended them to have.

## Small Group Bible Discovery (15 minutes)

> *Participant's Guide pages 32–38.*
>
> During this time, a group with fewer than seven participants will stay together. A group with seven or more participants will break into small groups and reassemble as a large group during the final five minutes. Assign each group one of the following topics. If you have more than four small groups, assign some topics to more than one group.

Let's break into groups of three to five—people sitting near you—and study some of the Bible passages and truths mentioned in the video.

Turn to pages 32–38 in your Participant's Guide. There you'll find a list of four topics. You'll have ten minutes to read and discuss the topic I'll assign to you. Choose one person in your group to be a spokesperson for your group when we discuss these topics later.

> Assign each group a topic.

I'll signal you when one minute is left.

## Topic A: The Battle Between Good and Evil

1.  What do the following Scripture passages reveal about God's motivation for wanting His people to control and influence strategic places such as Megiddo?

    a.  Isaiah 43:12

        *Suggested Response:* God desires that we will be His witnesses and proclaim to the world that He—and He alone—is God.

    b.  2 Kings 19:14–19

        *Suggested Response:* When the city of Jerusalem faced certain annihilation by the army of Sennacherib, the Assyrian king who had openly mocked God, King Hezekiah turned to God and asked Him to deliver the Israelites so that "all the kingdoms of the earth" would know that God alone was God.

2.  What did King Solomon do at Hazor, Megiddo, and Gezer—the three main cities along the Via Maris in Israel? (See 1 Kings 9:15–17.) Why?

    *Suggested Response:* Solomon fortified those cities because he recognized their importance. They were positioned at key spots along the Via Maris, so whoever controlled those cities controlled the international trade that passed through Israel.

3.  Megiddo has come to represent the battle between good and evil—the battle to influence culture. Consider the ways in which that battle has been highlighted by events at Megiddo.

## small Group Bible Discovery

### Topic A: The Battle Between Good and Evil

1.  What do the following Scripture passages reveal about God's motivation for wanting His people to control and influence strategic places such as Megiddo?

    a.  Isaiah 43:12

    b.  2 Kings 19:14–19

2.  What did King Solomon do at Hazor, Megiddo, and Gezer—the three main cities along the Via Maris in Israel? (See 1 Kings 9:15–17.) Why?

3.  Megiddo has come to represent the battle between good and evil—the battle to influence culture. Consider the ways in which that battle has been highlighted by events at Megiddo.

    a.  What does the "high place" at Megiddo, where Baal was worshiped, symbolize in that battle?

    b.  What great defeat for God's people took place at Megiddo? (See 2 Kings 23:29.)

a.  What does the "high place" at Megiddo, where Baal was worshiped, symbolize in that battle?

*Suggested Responses:* It stands as a testimony to the failure of God's people to influence their culture for God. It is an evidence of a sinful culture influencing God's people rather than God's people influencing the culture.

b.  What great defeat for God's people took place at Megiddo? (See 2 Kings 23:29.)

*Suggested Response:* King Josiah, who had greatly influenced the culture by leading Judah back to God, was killed in battle.

c.  Read Revelation 16:12–16. What is the significance of the Jewish author of Revelation locating the most decisive battle of the ages at Megiddo?

*Suggested Responses:* It is the ultimate battle between good and evil, the battle for ultimate control of the world.

**Baal Sacrifice Altar**

4.  Jesus, who grew up within a few miles of Megiddo and the Valley of Jezreel, made a profound impact on His culture. How did people respond to Jesus' actions? (See Matthew 15:29–31.)

*Suggested Response:* The people praised the God of Israel.

32          Faith Lessons on the Prophets and Kings of Israel

## small Group Bible Discovery

### Topic A: The Battle Between Good and Evil

1. What do the following Scripture passages reveal about God's motivation for wanting His people to control and influence strategic places such as Megiddo?

   a. Isaiah 43:12

   b. 2 Kings 19:14–19

2. What did King Solomon do at Hazor, Megiddo, and Gezer—the three main cities along the Via Maris in Israel? (See 1 Kings 9:15–17.) Why?

3. Megiddo has come to represent the battle between good and evil—the battle to influence culture. Consider the ways in which that battle has been highlighted by events at Megiddo.

   a. What does the "high place" at Megiddo, where Baal was worshiped, symbolize in that battle?

   b. What great defeat for God's people took place at Megiddo? (See 2 Kings 23:29.)

---

Session Two: Innocent Blood—Part 2                                   33

   c. Read Revelation 16:12–16. What is the significance of the Jewish author of Revelation locating the most decisive battle of the ages at Megiddo?

**Baal Sacrifice Altar**

4. Jesus, who grew up within a few miles of Megiddo and the Valley of Jezreel, made a profound impact on His culture. How did people respond to Jesus' actions? (See Matthew 15:29–31.)

## Topic B: God Has His Limits

1. God loves His people and is very patient with them. Sometimes, however, He cannot tolerate any more sin and brings judgment against those who spill innocent blood. Let's briefly review some of Israel's history to see how God responded to the faithful and unfaithful kings of His people after their nation split into two parts—Israel (ten northern tribes) and Judah.

   a. Hoshea of Israel—2 Kings 17:1–6, 9–18

   | Actions of the King/the People | God's Response |
   |---|---|
   | Hoshea did evil. The people rejected God's covenant and commands, did not listen to God's warnings, built high places and made idols, worshiped Baal, sacrificed their children, set up sacred stones and Asherah poles, practiced sorcery, etc. | God sent prophets to warn them, then He removed them from the land of Israel. The Assyrians imprisoned Hoshea, and after a three-year siege, captured the whole nation and carried everyone into exile in Assyria. |

   b. Hezekiah of Judah—2 Kings 18:1–8; 2 Chronicles 31:1

   | Actions of the King/the People | God's Response |
   |---|---|
   | King Hezekiah followed God and kept His commands. He had the people remove the high places, smash the pagan sacred stones, cut down the Asherah poles, and break the bronze snake that the people had been worshiping. | God was with King Hezekiah and enabled him to prosper. By the power of God, he refused to serve the king of Assyria and defeated the Philistines. |

   c. Manasseh, Hezekiah's son—2 Chronicles 33:1–6, 9–17

   | Actions of the King/the People | God's Response |
   |---|---|
   | He reinstituted pagan worship, rebuilt the high places, erected altars to Baal, made Asherah poles, worshiped stars, built pagan altars in the temple of the Lord, sacrificed his sons, practiced witchcraft, etc. But after he humbled himself and God restored his kingdom, he knew that the Lord was God, so he followed Him and commanded the people to do the same. | The Lord became very angry and sent the Assyrian army, which took Manasseh to Babylon, where he humbled himself before God. God then restored his kingdom. |

**Topic B: God Has His Limits**

1. God loves His people and is very patient with them. Sometimes, however, He cannot tolerate any more sin and brings judgment against those who spill innocent blood. Let's briefly review some of Israel's history to see how God responded to the faithful and unfaithful kings of His people after their nation split into two parts—Israel (ten northern tribes) and Judah.

   a. Hoshea of Israel—2 Kings 17:1–6, 9–18

   | Actions of the King/the People | God's Response |
   | --- | --- |
   |  |  |

   b. Hezekiah of Judah—2 Kings 18:1–8; 2 Chronicles 31:1

   | Actions of the King/the People | God's Response |
   | --- | --- |
   |  |  |

   c. Manasseh, Hezekiah's son—2 Chronicles 33:1–6, 9–17

   | Actions of the King/the People | God's Response |
   | --- | --- |
   |  |  |

d.  Amon, Hezekiah's grandson—2 Chronicles 33:21–23

| Actions of the King/the People | God's Response |
| --- | --- |
| He arrogantly worshiped and offered sacrifices to all the idols his father, Manasseh, had made, and did not humble himself before the Lord as his father had done. | Amon's guilt was multiplied, and God allowed his officials to assassinate him, although the people then killed those who had conspired against the king. |

e.  Josiah, Hezekiah's great-grandson—2 Chronicles 34:1–8, 30–33; 35:25–27

| Actions of the King/the People | God's Response |
| --- | --- |
| He followed God's commands and purged the land of high places, Asherah poles, Baal altars, false idols, etc. He then repaired the Lord's temple in Jerusalem, read the Book of the Covenant to the people, and had everyone pledge themselves to follow God's commands, which they did as long as he lived. | After Josiah was killed in battle, Jeremiah composed laments for him, and Josiah's acts of devotion to the Law of the Lord are recorded in Scripture. |

f.  Zedekiah—2 Chronicles 36:11–20

| Actions of the King/the People | God's Response |
| --- | --- |
| He did evil in the sight of God, refused to turn to God, and mocked God's prophets. The leaders, priests, and people also became more and more unfaithful, even defiling the temple of the Lord. | God pitied His people and sent them many warnings and messengers, but they despised His words and scoffed at His prophets until God's anger had no remedy. Finally God handed them over to the Babylonians. |

## Topic C: Mixing Righteousness with Evil

Soon after entering the Promised Land, the Israelites had to choose whether they would worship the God of Israel and/or the fertility gods of the Canaanites. Often the Israelites wavered between the two: first serving God, then sacrificing to Baal and Asherah, and sometimes worshiping both.

1.  Even before the Israelites crossed the Jordan River and entered the Promised Land, some of them had begun to worship the Canaanite gods. How did this come about, and what was God's response? (See Numbers 25:1–9.)

*Suggested Responses:* Some of the Israelite men had committed sexual immorality with Moabite women, who invited them to attend sacrifices to Canaanite gods; the Israelites then ate food at those sacrifices and bowed down before

d. Amon, Hezekiah's grandson—2 Chronicles 33:21–23

| Actions of the King/the People | God's Response |
|---|---|
| | |

e. Josiah, Hezekiah's great-grandson—2 Chronicles 34:1–8, 30–33; 35:25–27

| Actions of the King/the People | God's Response |
|---|---|
| | |

f. Zedekiah—2 Chronicles 36:11–20

| Actions of the King/the People | God's Response |
|---|---|
| | |

36 Faith Lessons on the Prophets and Kings of Israel

### Topic C: Mixing Righteousness with Evil

Soon after entering the Promised Land, the Israelites had to choose whether they would worship the God of Israel and/or the fertility gods of the Canaanites. Often the Israelites wavered between the two: first serving God, then sacrificing to Baal and Asherah, and sometimes worshiping both.

1. Even before the Israelites crossed the Jordan River and entered the Promised Land, some of them had begun to worship the Canaanite gods. How did this come about, and what was God's response? (See Numbers 25:1–9.)

2. What do each of the following passages reveal about the impact of pagan worship practices on Israel's culture and on God's dealings with His people?

   a. Judges 10:6–16

   b. 1 Kings 10:23–24; 11:1–11

   c. 2 Chronicles 33:1–13

   d. Jeremiah 19:3–6

   e. Ezekiel 23:36–39 (Oholah and Oholibah are names for Israel and Judah)

false gods. God became angry and, through Moses, commanded Israel's judges to kill the Baal-worshiping Israelites. God also sent a plague that killed about 24,000 Israelites. The plague stopped only when Phinehas killed an Israelite man and the Midianite woman he had brought into his tent for the purpose of sexual relations.

✏ 2. What do each of the following passages reveal about the impact of pagan worship practices on Israel's culture and on God's dealings with His people?

a. Judges 10:6–16

*Suggested Responses:* The Israelites forsook the Lord and worshiped the Canaanite gods, which made God angry. So He allowed various enemies to crush and oppress the Israelites until they cried out to Him and turned back to Him. When they confessed their sin, got rid of their foreign gods, and again began to serve Him, God delivered them from their misery.

b. 1 Kings 10:23–24; 11:1–11

*Suggested Responses:* The whole world sought after Solomon to hear God's wisdom. Yet even he, Israel's most influential king, was seduced into worshiping false gods through the encouragement of his many foreign wives. Although Solomon built and dedicated God's temple and had on two occasions received personal visits from God, he was not fully devoted to God and followed Baal (Molech) and Ashtoreth and even built a high place east of Jerusalem. Because of Solomon's unfaithfulness, God determined to break up the nation of Israel.

c. 2 Chronicles 33:1–13

*Suggested Responses:* King Manasseh completely rejected the worship of God that his father had reestablished in Judah. He engaged in all kinds of heathen worship, sorcery, and witchcraft and even erected an idol and built pagan altars in the holy temple of the Lord. The people paid no attention to God's warning call, so God allowed the Assyrians to capture him and take him to Babylon, where he repented and sought God. God then restored him to his kingdom.

d. Jeremiah 19:3–6

*Suggested Responses:* After the people had forsaken God and shed innocent blood in their worship of foreign gods—something that was appalling and intolerable to God—He sent Jeremiah to warn them of the punishment that would be coming.

e. Ezekiel 23:36–39 (Oholah and Oholibah are names for Israel and Judah)

*Suggested Responses:* God sent Ezekiel to confront the people concerning their detestable practices—not only the sacrifice of their children but their simultaneous worship of God that desecrated His house.

**Topic C: Mixing Righteousness with Evil**

Soon after entering the Promised Land, the Israelites had to choose whether they would worship the God of Israel and/or the fertility gods of the Canaanites. Often the Israelites wavered between the two: first serving God, then sacrificing to Baal and Asherah, and sometimes worshiping both.

1. Even before the Israelites crossed the Jordan River and entered the Promised Land, some of them had begun to worship the Canaanite gods. How did this come about, and what was God's response? (See Numbers 25:1–9.)

2. What do each of the following passages reveal about the impact of pagan worship practices on Israel's culture and on God's dealings with His people?

   a. Judges 10:6–16

   b. 1 Kings 10:23–24; 11:1–11

   c. 2 Chronicles 33:1–13

   d. Jeremiah 19:3–6

   e. Ezekiel 23:36–39 (Oholah and Oholibah are names for Israel and Judah)

## Topic D: Worship Practices of the Canaanites

The Canaanite religions can generally be categorized as fertility cults. In addition to seeking to appease the gods through sacrifices (sometimes human), the Canaanites practiced many types of sexual perversion as part of their worship of Baal and Asherah (Ashtoreth).

**The High Place and Altar at Dan**

1. What do the following verses reveal about the practices involved in the worship of Canaanite gods?

| Reference | Worship Practices |
|---|---|
| Deuteronomy 7:5–6 | involved the use of altars, sacred stones, Asherah poles, and idols |
| 1 Kings 14:24; 22:46 | involved male shrine prostitutes and what God described as detestable practices |
| Deuteronomy 23:17–18 | involved male and female shrine prostitutes |
| Isaiah 57:5–7; | involved high places, prostitution, child sacrifice, idolatry, |
| Ezekiel 16:20–21 | drink and grain offerings |
| 1 Chronicles 5:25 | worshipers prostituted themselves to the gods of the land |
| Hosea 4:10–14 | involved high places, prostitution, idolatry, and drinking |

2. What did the Israelites who worshiped Asherah have the audacity to do? (See 2 Kings 21:7; 23:7.)

*Suggested Responses:* They put up an Asherah pole in the temple of the Lord and made places in the temple for the male shrine prostitutes to live and for the women who did weaving for Asherah.

**Topic D: Worship Practices of the Canaanites**

The Canaanite religions can generally be categorized as fertility cults. In addition to seeking to appease the gods through sacrifices (sometimes human), the Canaanites practiced many types of sexual perversion as part of their worship of Baal and Asherah (Ashtoreth).

1. What do the following verses reveal about the practices involved in the worship of Canaanite gods?

| Reference | Worship Practices |
|---|---|
| Deuteronomy 7:5–6 | |
| 1 Kings 14:24; 22:46 | |
| Deuteronomy 23:17–18 | |
| Isaiah 57:5–7; Ezekiel 16:20–21 | |
| 1 Chronicles 5:25 | |
| Hosea 4:10–14 | |

**The High Place and Altar at Dan**

2. What did the Israelites who worshiped Asherah have the audacity to do? (See 2 Kings 21:7; 23:7.)

3. What image did God use to describe Israel and Judah's pursuit of the Canaanite gods? What message was He communicating by the use of that image? (See Jeremiah 3:6–14.)

4. What image did Ezekiel use to describe Israel and Judah's worship of the Canaanite gods? (See Ezekiel 23:1–4, 35–39.)

✎ 3. What image did God use to describe Israel and Judah's pursuit of the Canaanite gods? What message was He communicating by the use of that image? (See Jeremiah 3:6–14.)

*Suggested Responses:* God described their spiritual unfaithfulness in terms of physical adultery. Worship of Baal and Asherah was considered to be adultery against Yahweh, Israel's husband, in part because it involved immoral sexual practices.

✎ 4. What image did Ezekiel use to describe Israel and Judah's worship of the Canaanite gods? (See Ezekiel 23:1–4, 35–39.)

*Suggested Response:* Ezekiel gives both kingdoms symbolic names and labels them prostitutes because of their lust and seeking after other gods. He states the ways in which they were lewd, unfaithful, and adulterous in their relationship with God.

> After nine minutes, let participants know that they have one minute remaining. Then reassemble the entire group. After everyone is back together, begin asking one person from each small group to briefly share a key idea with the larger group. In some cases, you may not have time for every group to share its discoveries.

As time allows, let's briefly share the key ideas that your group discussed.

# faith Lesson

9 minutes       **Time for Reflection (4 minutes)**

It's time for each of us to think quietly about what we've learned today and how the battle to influence culture for God applies to us, to our place in our culture. On page 39 of your Participant's Guide, you'll find a passage of Scripture. Read this passage silently and then consider the questions that follow.

Please do not talk during this time. It's a time when we all can reflect on how the message of this video applies to our lives.

> *The Scripture passage and questions are reproduced in their entirety in the Participant's Guide on pages 39–40.*

The Lord said to me: "Son of man, will you judge Oholah and Oholibah [Israel and Judah]? Then confront them with their detestable practices, for they have committed adultery and blood is on their hands. They committed adultery with their idols; they even sacrificed their children, whom they bore to me, as food for them. They have also done this to me: At that same time they defiled my sanctuary and desecrated my Sabbaths. On the very day they sacrificed their children to their idols, they entered my sanctuary and desecrated it. That is what they did in my house...." This is what the Sovereign Lord says: "Bring a mob against them and give them over to terror and plunder...."

2. What did the Israelites who worshiped Asherah have the audacity to do? (See 2 Kings 21:7; 23:7.)

3. What image did God use to describe Israel and Judah's pursuit of the Canaanite gods? What message was He communicating by the use of that image? (See Jeremiah 3:6–14.)

4. What image did Ezekiel use to describe Israel and Judah's worship of the Canaanite gods? (See Ezekiel 23:1–4, 35–39.)

## faith lesson

### Time for Reflection

Read the following passage of Scripture and take a few minutes to consider the ways in which the battle to influence culture for God applies to you and your place in culture.

> The LORD said to me: "Son of man, will you judge Oholah and Oholibah [Israel and Judah]? Then confront them with their detestable practices, for they have committed adultery and blood is on their hands. They committed adultery with their idols; they even sacrificed their children, whom they bore to me, as food for them. They have also done this to me: At that same time they defiled my sanctuary and desecrated my Sabbaths. On the very day they sacrificed their children to their idols, they entered my sanctuary and desecrated it. That is what they did in my house...." This is what the Sovereign LORD says: "Bring a mob against them and give them over to terror and plunder.... You will suffer the penalty for your lewdness and bear the consequences of your sins of idolatry. Then you will know that I am the Sovereign LORD."
>
> EZEKIEL 23:36–39, 46, 49

1. What must God do to get *your* attention so that you will know that He is God?

You will suffer the penalty for your lewdness and bear the consequences of your sins of idolatry. Then you will know that I am the Sovereign LORD."

EZEKIEL 23:36–39, 46, 49

1. What must God do to get *your* attention so that you will know that He is God?

2. There is a spiritual battle between good and evil taking place all around you for the hearts, minds, and souls of people.

   a. Where are your allegiances in this battle?

   b. How deep are your loyalties?

   c. For which cause do you expend your efforts?

## Action Points (5 minutes)

> *The following points are reproduced on pages 40–42 of the Participant's Guide:*

Now it's time to wrap up our session.

> **Give participants a moment to transition from their thoughtfulness to giving you their full attention.**

I'd like to take a moment to summarize the key points we explored. After I have reviewed these points, I will give you a moment to jot down an action step (or steps) that you will commit to this week as a result of what you have learned today.

> **Read the following points and pause after each so that participants can consider and write out their commitment.**

1. Located above the Valley of Jezreel, Megiddo stood guard over the Via Maris at a key mountain pass: whoever controlled the city controlled the trade route. Within sight of that city, terrible battles took place in the Plain of Jezreel. *Today, as in ancient Israel, great spiritual battles are taking place throughout the world between the people of God and the people of evil, between the values of God and the values of Satan. They are battles for the hearts, minds, and souls of people—and the consequences are great.*

   **What do you think God feels when He looks at the culture in which you live? Why?**

   **Where is your "Megiddo"—the center of influence where God has placed you? What has God given you to accomplish there?**

   **Can you identify another "Megiddo"—perhaps a more powerful center of influence within your culture—that God might be preparing you to influence for Him in the future?**

# ꜰaith Lesson

**Time for Reflection**

Read the following passage of Scripture and take a few minutes to consider the ways in which the battle to influence culture for God applies to you and your place in culture.

> The LORD said to me: "Son of man, will you judge Oholah and Oholibah [Israel and Judah]? Then confront them with their detestable practices, for they have committed adultery and blood is on their hands. They committed adultery with their idols; they even sacrificed their children, whom they bore to me, as food for them. They have also done this to me: At that same time they defiled my sanctuary and desecrated my Sabbaths. On the very day they sacrificed their children to their idols, they entered my sanctuary and desecrated it. That is what they did in my house...." This is what the Sovereign LORD says: "Bring a mob against them and give them over to terror and plunder.... You will suffer the penalty for your lewdness and bear the consequences of your sins of idolatry. Then you will know that I am the Sovereign LORD."
>
> EZEKIEL 23:36–39, 46, 49

1. What must God do to get *your* attention so that you will know that He is God?

2. There is a spiritual battle between good and evil taking place all around you for the hearts, minds, and souls of people.

   a. Where are your allegiances in this battle?

   b. How deep are your loyalties?

   c. For which cause do you expend your efforts?

**Action Points**

Take a moment to review the key points you explored today. Then jot down an action step (or steps) that you will commit to this week as a result of what you have learned today.

1. Located above the Valley of Jezreel, Megiddo stood guard over the Via Maris at a key mountain pass: whoever controlled the city controlled the trade route. Within sight of that city, terrible battles took place in the Plain of Jezreel. *Today, as in ancient Israel, great spiritual battles are taking place throughout the world between the people of God and the people of evil, between the values of God and the values of Satan. They are battles for the hearts, minds, and souls of people—and the consequences are great.*

   What do you think God feels when He looks at the culture in which you live? Why?

2. *The Israelites were called to serve God, who loves innocence. But during King Ahab's reign, while they claimed to worship God, they also worshiped the evil gods of Canaan (especially Baal) and sacrificed their children for personal gain.* God strongly condemned their claim to honor Him while they engaged in such abominable practices.

Today, we face similar choices. How easy it can be to honor God, on the one hand, and yet allow sinful patterns of thought and action to remain rooted in our lives. How easy it can be to sacrifice others in order to gain personal blessing and achieve "success."

**In what way(s) might you be sacrificing who God wants you to be or what He wants you to do in order to attain personal "success"?**

**In what ways are you actively fighting for God and His values against the forces of evil? Conversely, in what ways do your actions or motivations undermine the purity of your heart before God?**

**What practical steps will you take to seek purity before God and to honor Him in everything you do, say, and think?**

3. *Megiddo also stands as a symbol of hope and promise.* It reminds us that the battle between good and evil is ultimately the battle for control of the world. Because of the redemptive work of Jesus Christ, those who engage in the battle against evil can take heart. For when the battle is finally over, Jesus Christ will be the victor. He will be crowned King of Kings!

**As you face the battle to influence your culture—your Megiddo—for God, what frightens or threatens you?**

**In what ways does the certainty of Jesus' victory encourage you?**

**The Valley of Jezreel Viewed Across the Altar of Megiddo**

Session Two: Innocent Blood—Part 2     41

Where is your "Megiddo"—the center of influence where God has placed you? What has God given you to accomplish there?

Can you identify another "Megiddo"—perhaps a more powerful center of influence within your culture—that God might be preparing you to influence for Him in the future?

2. *The Israelites were called to serve God, who loves innocence. But during King Ahab's reign, while they claimed to worship God, they also worshiped the evil gods of Canaan (especially Baal) and sacrificed their children for personal gain.* God strongly condemned their claim to honor Him while they engaged in such abominable practices.

Today, we face similar choices. How easy it can be to honor God, on the one hand, and yet allow sinful patterns of thought and action to remain rooted in our lives. How easy it can be to sacrifice others in order to gain personal blessing and achieve "success."

In what way(s) might you be sacrificing who God wants you to be or what He wants you to do in order to attain personal "success"?

---

42         Faith Lessons on the Prophets and Kings of Israel

In what ways are you actively fighting for God and His values against the forces of evil? Conversely, in what ways do your actions or motivations undermine the purity of your heart before God?

What practical steps will you take to seek purity before God and to honor Him in everything you do, say, and think?

3. *Megiddo also stands as a symbol of hope and promise.* It reminds us that the battle between good and evil is ultimately the battle for control of the world. Because of the redemptive work of Jesus Christ, those who engage in the battle against evil can take heart. For when the battle is finally over, Jesus Christ will be the victor. He will be crowned King of Kings!

As you face the battle to influence your culture—your Megiddo—for God, what frightens or threatens you?

In what ways does the certainty of Jesus' victory encourage you?

**PLANNING NOTES:**

**AUTHOR'S RECOMMENDATION**

I strongly recommend that participants read the well-written and exciting book, *Roaring Lambs: A Gentle Plan to Radically Change Your World* by Bob Briner. He believes that the Christian community has failed to participate in institutions and activities that have the greatest influence on culture. Citing extensive examples of Christians' failure to participate in movies, television, literature, and the visual arts, Bob presents an interesting proposal to encourage young Christians to pursue careers in those fields.

His specific suggestions include ways to support young people and encourage them to follow God's call into those fields; how to influence television programming and encourage production of good literature; and how to encourage colleges to prepare people to be influential in those important fields. Since he is speaking about the areas we have called the "Megiddos" of culture, his book offers excellent, practical applications of this concept.

# closing prayer

**2** minutes

I hope that this session has challenged you, as it has me, to think about the spiritual influence we can have on the "Megiddos" of our culture and to consider the ways in which we are not pure in heart and may even sacrifice the wrong things to gain personal success. Let's close in prayer.

*Dear God, You know the battles in which each of us is involved today—battles that truly make a difference to our families, communities, and country. Please give us the courage to influence the Megiddos of our culture so that they will reflect more of You and Your values. Make us aware of the sins we harbor while we outwardly worship You. Give us the strength and courage to resist the seductive gods of our culture—fame, money, relationships. Draw us close to You so that we may resist these gods. In Your name we pray, amen.*

**DATA FILE**

**Water Systems of Old Testament Times**

Because Israel is an arid country, water has always been important to its inhabitants. In the ancient Near East, cities were built only where fresh water existed. People spent a good part of their day obtaining water for their needs.

When a city was small, a nearby spring, well, or cistern was sufficient. But as a city grew, its inhabitants took steps to protect their water supply from threatening armies. During Solomon's time, a wall or corridor often extended from the city wall to the nearby spring or well. But this setup was vulnerable to extended sieges.

During the late ninth or early eighth century B.C., a new technology emerged: the water shaft. People would dig a shaft to reach the water table

(continued on page 68)

**The Valley of Jezreel Viewed Across the Altar of Megiddo**

### AUTHOR'S RECOMMENDATION

I strongly recommend that participants read the well-written and exciting book, *Roaring Lambs: A Gentle Plan to Radically Change Your World* by Bob Briner. He believes that the Christian community has failed to participate in institutions and activities that have the greatest influence on culture. Citing extensive examples of Christians' failure to participate in movies, television, literature, and the visual arts, Bob presents an interesting proposal to encourage young Christians to pursue careers in those fields.

His specific suggestions include ways to support young people and encourage them to follow God's call into those fields; how to influence television programming and encourage production of good literature; and how to encourage colleges to prepare people to be influential in those important fields. Since he is speaking about the areas we have called the "Megiddos" of culture, his book offers excellent, practical applications of this concept.

### DATA FILE

**Water Systems of Old Testament Times**

Because Israel is an arid country, water has always been important to its inhabitants. In the ancient Near East, cities were built only where fresh water existed. People spent a good part of their day obtaining water for their needs.

When a city was small, a nearby spring, well, or cistern was sufficient. But as a city grew, its inhabitants took steps to protect their water supply from threatening armies. During Solomon's time, a wall or corridor often extended from the city wall to the nearby spring or well. But this setup was vulnerable to extended sieges.

During the late ninth or early eighth century B.C., a new technology emerged: the water shaft. People would dig a shaft to reach the water table and—sometimes using a horizontal tunnel, too—would direct the water into the city. During Hezekiah's reign, for example, a tunnel system allowed water from a spring outside Jerusalem to flow through the mountain ridge on which the city was built and into a pool inside the city walls.

**The Entrance to the Water Shaft on Tel Megiddo**

Scholars believe that sometime during the ninth century B.C., the inhabitants of Megiddo dug a square, vertical shaft more than 115 feet deep that connected to a horizontal tunnel. This tunnel traveled nearly 220 feet underneath the city to the cave in which a spring—the

(continued from page 66)

and—sometimes using a horizontal tunnel, too—would direct the water into the city. During Hezekiah's reign, for example, a tunnel system allowed water from a spring outside Jerusalem to flow through the mountain ridge on which the city was built and into a pool inside the city walls.

Scholars believe that sometime during the ninth century B.C., the inhabitants of Megiddo dug a square, vertical shaft more than 115 feet deep that connected to a horizontal tunnel. This tunnel traveled nearly 220 feet underneath the city to the cave in which a spring—the city's water source—was located. Evidently one crew began digging in the cave, the other at the bottom of the shaft inside the city. When the builders met in the middle, they had accomplished one of the engineering wonders of the world! The cave was then sealed from the outside, securing the water supply from enemy attack. Every day women descended the steps that wound around the outside walls of the shaft and walked through the tunnel to the spring.

**The Entrance to the Water Shaft on Tel Megiddo**

**The Ancient Wall Blocking the Cave of the Spring at Megiddo (Outside View)**

**The Water Tunnel of Megiddo**

## DATA FILE

### Water Systems of Old Testament Times

Because Israel is an arid country, water has always been important to its inhabitants. In the ancient Near East, cities were built only where fresh water existed. People spent a good part of their day obtaining water for their needs.

When a city was small, a nearby spring, well, or cistern was sufficient. But as a city grew, its inhabitants took steps to protect their water supply from threatening armies. During Solomon's time, a wall or corridor often extended from the city wall to the nearby spring or well. But this setup was vulnerable to extended sieges.

During the late ninth or early eighth century B.C., a new technology emerged: the water shaft. People would dig a shaft to reach the water table and—sometimes using a horizontal tunnel, too—would direct the water into the city. During Hezekiah's reign, for example, a tunnel system allowed water from a spring outside Jerusalem to flow through the mountain ridge on which the city was built and into a pool inside the city walls.

The Entrance to the Water Shaft on Tel Megiddo

Scholars believe that sometime during the ninth century B.C., the inhabitants of Megiddo dug a square, vertical shaft more than 115 feet deep that connected to a horizontal tunnel. This tunnel traveled nearly 220 feet underneath the city to the cave in which a spring—the

city's water source—was located. Evidently one crew began digging in the cave, the other at the bottom of the shaft inside the city. When the builders met in the middle, they had accomplished one of the engineering wonders of the world! The cave was then sealed from the outside, securing the water supply from enemy attack. Every day women descended the steps that wound around the outside walls of the shaft and walked through the tunnel to the spring.

The Ancient Wall Blocking the Cave of the Spring at Megiddo (Outside View)

The Water Tunnel of Megiddo

PLANNING NOTES:

## THE EVIDENCE OF TIME

### How to Tell a Tel

Israel is a land of hills and mountains. In fact, a first-time visitor often is amazed by how little flat land there is. Most travelers also notice that Israel is dotted with a distinctive type of hill that has steep sides, a flat top, and looks a bit like a coffee table—especially when it is located in a valley and is viewed from above. Such a hill is called a *tel*, and tels are particularly important to Bible students.

A tel comprises layers and layers of ruined settlements that have been rebuilt on top of the ruins of previous settlements. In general terms, here's how tels such as Tel Megiddo were formed.

#### Stage 1

People settled on the site, eventually building a wall and gate. The king or rulers would build a palace and a temple, and the people would build houses inside the city walls. Often a steeply sloped rampart was built against the wall to protect the hill from erosion and to keep enemies away from the base of the wall. Over time, the ramparts were replaced or covered with others. These buried walls and ramparts gave the hill its steep, straight shape.

#### Stage 2

As the city grew and prospered, it became an attractive prize. Enemies would lay siege to it, sometimes penetrating the defenses and killing its inhabitants. Armies were usually brutally destructive in their conquests. Occasionally enemies remained to occupy the city, but usually they marched off, leaving behind smoking ruins.

Because of droughts, wars, or other reasons, once-prosperous cities were sometimes abandoned. Sand carried by the relentless winds of the Middle East gradually covered what remained of the houses and streets. Nomads would pitch their tents on the site, then move on. Soon the ruins blended into the landscape.

#### Stage 3

Even when a city was destroyed or vacated, the three conditions necessary for establishing a settlement in that place usually remained—a water source or adequate rainfall, an occupation that could generate a consistent food supply, and a defensible location. So, eventually people resettled on the same site. Lacking the heavy equipment needed to remove the debris left by previous inhabitants, the newcomers filled in holes, gathered larger building stones, leveled off the top of the hill, and rebuilt. Soon another prosperous community developed. Inevitably, its success attracted enemies . . . and the cycle of destruction and rebuilding resumed.

(continued on page 72)

## THE EVIDENCE OF TIME

### How to Tell a Tel

Israel is a land of hills and mountains. In fact, a first-time visitor often is amazed by how little flat land there is. Most travelers also notice that Israel is dotted with a distinctive type of hill that has steep sides, a flat top, and looks a bit like a coffee table—especially when it is located in a valley and is viewed from above. Such a hill is called a *tel*, and tels are particularly important to Bible students.

A tel comprises layers and layers of ruined settlements that have been rebuilt on top of the ruins of previous settlements. In general terms, here's how tels such as Tel Megiddo were formed.

#### Stage 1

People settled on the site, eventually building a wall and gate. The king or rulers would build a palace and a temple, and the people would build houses inside the city walls. Often a steeply sloped rampart was built against the wall to protect the hill from erosion and to keep enemies away from the base of the wall. Over time, the ramparts were replaced or covered with others. These buried walls and ramparts gave the hill its steep, straight shape.

#### Stage 2

As the city grew and prospered, it became an attractive prize. Enemies would lay siege to it, sometimes penetrating the defenses and killing its inhabitants. Armies were usually brutally destructive in their conquests. Occasionally enemies remained to occupy the city, but usually they marched off, leaving behind smoking ruins.

Because of droughts, wars, or other reasons, once-prosperous cities were sometimes abandoned. Sand carried by the relentless winds of the Middle East gradually covered what remained of the houses and streets. Nomads would pitch their tents on the site, then move on. Soon the ruins blended into the landscape.

#### Stage 3

Even when a city was destroyed or vacated, the three conditions necessary for establishing a settlement in that place usually remained—a water source or adequate rainfall, an occupation that could generate a

consistent food supply, and a defensible location. So, eventually people resettled on the same site. Lacking the heavy equipment needed to remove the debris left by previous inhabitants, the newcomers filled in holes, gathered larger building stones, leveled off the top of the hill, and rebuilt. Soon another prosperous community developed. Inevitably, its success attracted enemies . . . and the cycle of destruction and rebuilding resumed.

Tel Beth Shean

#### Stage 4

Over centuries—even millennia—layers upon layers of settlements accumulated (sort of like a layer cake), so the hill became higher and higher. Each layer—or stratum—records what life was like during the time of a particular settlement. Jerusalem has at least twenty-one layers, and Megiddo has even more. Locked within these layers are artifacts such as pottery, jewelry, weapons, documents, gates, temples, palaces, and houses—all of which are waiting for archaeologists to uncover their stories and discover how the people of those settlements lived.

Artifacts unearthed at Tel Megiddo and other tels enable us to know how people lived during biblical times: what they ate, how they worshiped, what their customs were, and many other important details. Each tel is, in effect, a unique gift from God that helps make ancient times more relevant to us today and helps us better understand the Bible's message.

(continued from page 70)

### Stage 4

Over centuries—even millennia —layers upon layers of settlements accumulated (sort of like a layer cake), so the hill became higher and higher. Each layer—or stratum—records what life was like during the time of a particular settlement. Jerusalem has at least twenty-one layers, and Megiddo has even more. Locked within these layers are artifacts such as pottery, jewelry, weapons, documents, gates, temples, palaces, and houses—all of which are waiting for archaeologists to uncover their stories and discover how the people of those settlements lived.

**Tel Beth Shean**

Artifacts unearthed at Tel Megiddo and other tels enable us to know how people lived during biblical times: what they ate, how they worshiped, what their customs were, and many other important details. Each tel is, in effect, a unique gift from God that helps make ancient times more relevant to us today and helps us better understand the Bible's message.

consistent food supply, and a defensible location. So, eventually people resettled on the same site. Lacking the heavy equipment needed to remove the debris left by previous inhabitants, the newcomers filled in holes, gathered larger building stones, leveled off the top of the hill, and rebuilt. Soon another prosperous community developed. Inevitably, its success attracted enemies...and the cycle of destruction and rebuilding resumed.

**Tel Beth Shean**

### Stage 4

Over centuries—even millennia—layers upon layers of settlements accumulated (sort of like a layer cake), so the hill became higher and higher. Each layer—or stratum—records what life was like during the time of a particular settlement. Jerusalem has at least twenty-one layers, and Megiddo has even more. Locked within these layers are artifacts such as pottery, jewelry, weapons, documents, gates, temples, palaces, and houses—all of which are waiting for archaeologists to uncover their stories and discover how the people of those settlements lived.

Artifacts unearthed at Tel Megiddo and other tels enable us to know how people lived during biblical times: what they ate, how they worshiped, what their customs were, and many other important details. Each tel is, in effect, a unique gift from God that helps make ancient times more relevant to us today and helps us better understand the Bible's message.

## FACT FILE

### Three Essential Conditions

The environment of the Middle East, including Israel, is harsh and mostly unsuitable for settlement. For a location such as Megiddo to be habitable, three conditions were needed.

#### Fresh Water

Although rainfall is plentiful in some regions of Israel, most rain falls during the winter. During ancient times, many communities stored rainwater in cisterns. If rainfall was below average, cisterns dried up and people abandoned their city. If an enemy laid siege to a city, only the cisterns inside the city walls were available to the people, and the water often ran out, causing the city to fall. Jerusalem was built next to the spring of Gihon. The residents of Megiddo, Hazor, and Gezer dug tunnels through bedrock to reach fresh water. Without an abundant water supply, no settlement could grow.

#### Profitable Occupation

People needed the opportunity to either grow a consistent food supply or be able to buy food.

- Olive trees flourished in Judea and Galilee.
- Wheat grew in the valleys of Judea and the Valley of Jezreel.
- Shepherds raised sheep and goats in the wilderness.
- Chorazin and Ekron had large, olive-oil processing facilities.
- Jerusalem was famous for its purple dye.
- Some cities supplied travelers using the Via Maris, the major trade route through the country.

#### A Defensible Location

The political climate in the Middle East was volatile, so cities typically were built on hills ringing fertile valleys so the inhabitants could defend themselves. Jerusalem, for example, was initially built on a long, narrow hill and then spread across a valley and encompassed another hill. Azekah was situated on a hill overlooking the Elah Valley, the site of David's confrontation with Goliath.

## FACT FILE

### Three Essential Conditions

The environment of the Middle East, including Israel, is harsh and mostly unsuitable for settlement. For a location such as Megiddo to be habitable, three conditions were needed.

#### Fresh Water

Although rainfall is plentiful in some regions of Israel, most rain falls during the winter. During ancient times, many communities stored rainwater in cisterns. If rainfall was below average, cisterns dried up and people abandoned their city. If an enemy laid siege to a city, only the cisterns inside the city walls were available to the people, and the water often ran out, causing the city to fall. Jerusalem was built next to the spring of Gihon. The residents of Megiddo, Hazor, and Gezer dug tunnels through bedrock to reach fresh water. Without an abundant water supply, no settlement could grow.

#### Profitable Occupation

People needed the opportunity to either grow a consistent food supply or be able to buy food.

- Olive trees flourished in Judea and Galilee.
- Wheat grew in the valleys of Judea and the Valley of Jezreel.
- Shepherds raised sheep and goats in the wilderness.
- Chorazin and Ekron had large, olive-oil processing facilities.
- Jerusalem was famous for its purple dye.
- Some cities supplied travelers using the Via Maris, the major trade route through the country.

#### A Defensible Location

The political climate in the Middle East was volatile, so cities typically were built on hills ringing fertile valleys so the inhabitants could defend themselves. Jerusalem, for example, was initially built on a long, narrow hill and then spread across a valley and encompassed another hill. Azekah was situated on a hill overlooking the Elah Valley, the site of David's confrontation with Goliath.

PLANNING NOTES:

# who is god?

## before you lead

### Synopsis

Today's session highlights a confrontation on the top of Mount Carmel between Elijah, the first of the great prophets of God who were sent to speak on God's behalf and to turn the hearts of the people of Israel back toward God, and 850 prophets of Baal and Asherah.

Although God had demonstrated Himself to the Israelites over and over again, they were unwilling to live in the Promised Land as God had called them to live. Over time, they became increasingly confused about who God was, and the Canaanite gods became increasingly attractive to them. By the time of Elijah, King Ahab and his wife, Jezebel, had introduced the Baal cult into everyday life. Following their king's example, the Israelites willingly compromised their beliefs and values concerning God and pursued Baal. Their dalliance with Baal worship, which included glorifying human sexuality and even sacrificing their children, was a stumbling block in their role of bringing about God's plan of salvation.

Both the location and timing of Elijah's encounter with the false prophets were strategic. Mount Carmel, which literally means *God's vineyard,* is the most heavily forested area of Israel. It receives about thirty inches of rain per year and overlooks the fertile Jezreel Valley—the breadbasket of ancient Israel. In Scripture, Mount Carmel repeatedly symbolizes fertility and blessing. In addition, the Via Maris, the trade route between the great empires of Assyria and Babylon to the east and Egypt to the southwest, passed by Mount Carmel through the Jezreel Valley. So Mount Carmel was the high point of a strategic area of fertility and influence.

At this time in Israel's history (about 850 B.C.), Solomon had died and the nation had been broken into two kingdoms—the northern nation of Israel (comprised of ten tribes) and the southern nation of Judah (comprised of two tribes). King Ahab, son of Omri, was king of Israel. Although Ahab gave his sons names that included part of God's name, he did evil in God's sight. Not only did Ahab marry a Baal priestess from Phoenicia named Jezebel who hated Israel's God, he set up an altar in a temple he built to honor Baal, made an Asherah pole, "and did more to provoke the LORD, the God of Israel, to anger than did all the kings of Israel before him" (1 Kings 16:33).

Into this scene came Elijah, a prophet whose name means "*Yahweh\* is God.*" Elijah told Ahab that there wouldn't be any rain or dew in Israel for years (1 Kings 17:1). By doing so, Elijah confronted Baal, the supposed god of rain. He said, in effect, "God is more powerful than the best thing you believe Baal has to offer." The ensuing drought created a crisis for Baal worshipers: was Baal really the true god of the land, who brought fertility, or was Jehovah the true God?

---

\* Or Jehovah.

Three and a half years later, God again told Elijah to go to Ahab. The prophet then called a meeting on Mount Carmel between himself, the people of Israel, and 850 false prophets of Baal and Asherah. At the start of that meeting, he challenged the Israelites by saying, "How long will you waver between two opinions? If the LORD is God, follow him; but if Baal is God, follow him" (1 Kings 18:21).

Elijah knew that the Israelites had not completely rejected the God of their fathers, but that they had chosen to worship Baal also. So he confronted them with God's demand for total allegiance. He challenged their loyalty to Yahweh in much the same way that Joshua challenged the Israelites years earlier: "But if serving the LORD seems undesirable to you," Joshua had said, "then choose for yourselves this day whom you will serve" (Joshua 24:15a). Joshua knew that since there was only one God, the Israelites could choose to serve Him or not. But when Elijah posed the question, the people said nothing!

So Elijah asked the prophets of Baal to call to their god and ask him to burn up the offering of a bull. Despite their frantic efforts, Baal didn't answer. After making fun of them and Baal, Elijah repaired the broken altar of the Lord using twelve stones (one for each tribe of Israel) and placed the bull upon it. After the Israelites completely doused his sacrifice with water, Elijah called upon God. "Answer me, O LORD," he prayed, "answer me, so these people will know that you, O LORD, are God, and that you are turning their hearts back again" (1 Kings 18:37).

In response, God sent His fire down. It burned up the sacrifice, the altar, the water, even the surrounding earth, and the Israelites cried out, "Yahweh, he is God!" In their own words, they cried out, "Elijah! Elijah!" They had seen Elijah in action and immediately recognized God. After the Baal prophets had been killed, Elijah prayed and God sent rain. Eventually, however, many of the Israelites reverted to Baal worship, and Elijah had to run for his life. But he had done what God had called him to do, and the people saw that Yahweh truly was God.

## Key Points of This Lesson

1. *God demands that we recognize that He alone is Lord of our lives.* He calls us to follow Him obediently and not to waver. We are to serve Him wholeheartedly and not to trust in other gods.

   When Elijah challenged the Israelites to stop wavering between God and Baal, they were silent. Indeed, they didn't stand up for God until after He sent fire down from heaven that burned up Elijah's sacrifice and the altar on which it stood. In contrast, when Joshua challenged the Israelites years earlier to evaluate whom they would serve (Joshua 24:15), they resoundingly said that they would serve the Lord.

2. *When we live out who God has made us to be, people will see God.* Elijah, whose very name meant *Yahweh is God*, did what God called him to do, and the people saw the evidence of God in a powerful way. When the Israelites recognized who God was, they (for a time) renounced Baal and killed the prophets of Baal and Asherah.

### Session Outline (53 minutes)

I. **Introduction** (4 minutes)
Welcome
What's to Come
Questions to Think About

II. **Show Video "Who Is God?"** (21 minutes)

III. **Group Discovery** (20 minutes)
Video Highlights
Small Group Bible Discovery

IV. **Faith Lesson** (7 minutes)
Time for Reflection
Action Points

V. **Closing Prayer** (1 minute)

## Materials

No additional materials are needed for this session. Simply view the video prior to leading the session so you are familiar with its main points.

# who is god?

## introduction

4 minutes

### Welcome

Assemble the participants together. Welcome them to session three of *Faith Lessons on the Prophets and Kings of Israel.*

### What's to Come

Although God had demonstrated Himself to the Israelites over and over again, they were unwilling to live as God had called them to live. Over time, they became increasingly confused about who God was, and the Canaanite gods became increasingly attractive to them. Today's session highlights a confrontation on the top of Mount Carmel between Elijah—the first of the great prophets of God who were sent to speak on God's behalf and to turn the hearts of the Israelites back toward God—and 850 prophets of Baal and Asherah. We'll see how Elijah's actions enabled people to see God in a powerful way. We, too, will be challenged to follow God without wavering and to live in ways that proclaim to other people that Jehovah is God.

### Questions to Think About

*Participant's Guide page 49.*

Ask each question and solicit a few responses from group members.

1. What kinds of situations can tempt us to lose faith in God and pursue other "gods" that we think will make our lives better?

   *Suggested Responses:* Difficult situations such as financial setbacks, sickness, problems with a family member, etc., can cause us to lose faith in God. Situations such as fame, increasing income, a great career, etc., can do this as well. When we take our eyes off God and allow our faith in Him to waver, other things can easily take His place.

2. Describe a situation in which you felt pulled between two opposing values and had a difficult time choosing one over the other. What did you feel? How did you eventually make your decision?

   *Suggested Responses:* Allow participants to share their experiences and encourage them to describe their feelings—uncertainty, fear, insecurity, loneliness, etc.—as well as what finally pushed them to decide one way or another.

SESSION THREE

# who is god?

## questions to think about

1. What kinds of situations can tempt us to lose faith in God and pursue other "gods" that we think will make our lives better?

2. Describe a situation in which you felt pulled between two opposing values and had a difficult time choosing one over the other. What did you feel? How did you eventually make your decision?

3. Think about a godly person you know who reflects God in everything he or she does. What about that person communicates that the Lord is God? What effect does that person have on others?

49

✏ 3.    Think about a godly person you know who reflects God in everything he or she does. What about that person communicates that the Lord is God? What effect does that person have on others?

*Suggested Responses:* Allow participants to share what they have observed in others.

Let's keep these ideas in mind as we view the video.

# video presentation

2I minutes

*Participant's Guide page 50.*

On page 50 of your Participant's Guide, you will find a space in which to take notes on key points as we watch this video.

## Leader's Video Observations

The Geographical Setting—Mount Carmel

The Historical Setting—King Ahab

Elijah—His Name, His Mission

The Confrontation on Mount Carmel

**SESSION THREE**

# who is god?

## questions to think about

1. What kinds of situations can tempt us to lose faith in God and pursue other "gods" that we think will make our lives better?

2. Describe a situation in which you felt pulled between two opposing values and had a difficult time choosing one over the other. What did you feel? How did you eventually make your decision?

3. Think about a godly person you know who reflects God in everything he or she does. What about that person communicates that the Lord is God? What effect does that person have on others?

49

## video notes

**The Geographical Setting—Mount Carmel**

**The Historical Setting—King Ahab**

**Elijah—His Name, His Mission**

**The Confrontation on Mount Carmel**

# group Discovery

20 minutes

> If your group has seven or more members, use the **Video Highlights** with the entire group (5 minutes), then break into small groups of three to five to discuss the **Small Group Bible Discovery** (10 minutes). Then reassemble the group to discuss the key points discovered (5 minutes).
>
> If your group has fewer than seven members, begin with the **Video Highlights** (5 minutes), then do one or more of the topics found in the **Small Group Bible Discovery** as a group (10 minutes). Finally, spend five minutes at the end discussing points that had an impact on participants.

## Video Highlights (5 minutes)

> Here you'll ask one or more of the following questions that directly relate to the video the participants have just seen.

1. What effect did King Ahab's leadership have on the Israelites?

   *Suggested Responses:* King Ahab did many evil things, including setting up a temple honoring Baal and marrying a pagan woman who worshiped Baal and hated the God of Israel. His example, and that of his wife, made Baal worship an everyday part of life in Israel.

2. Why is the meaning of Elijah's name significant in light of his confrontation with the prophets of Baal on Mount Carmel?

   *Suggested Responses:* Elijah's name meant "Yahweh is God." After the Baal and Asherah prophets tried unsuccessfully to call down fire from heaven, Elijah prayed that God would let it be known that He was God in Israel. After God answered Elijah's prayer on Mount Carmel, the people cried out, "Elijah! Elijah!"

3. What did the three-and-a-half-year-long drought communicate to the Israelites, whose faith was wavering between God and Baal? What is the significance of the fact that the drought ended after Elijah prayed?

   *Suggested Responses:* The drought demonstrated that God was much more powerful than Baal, the fertility god who supposedly caused rain to fall. The fact that the drought ended after Elijah prayed showed that Elijah's power was a result of his personal relationship with God.

4. What circumstances or responses of the people indicate that the Israelites were confused as to which god was the true God?

   *Suggested Responses:* the fact that the altar of the Lord was in disrepair, the people's refusal to answer Elijah's question regarding their allegiance to God, the great number of Baal and Asherah prophets vs. the one prophet of God, etc.

## video нighlights

1. What effect did King Ahab's leadership have on the Israelites?

2. Why is the meaning of Elijah's name significant in light of his confrontation with the prophets of Baal on Mount Carmel?

3. What did the three-and-a-half-year-long drought communicate to the Israelites, whose faith was wavering between God and Baal? What is the significance of the fact that the drought ended after Elijah prayed?

4. What circumstances or responses of the people indicate that the Israelites were confused as to which god was the true God?

PLANNING NOTES:

## WHY MOUNT CARMEL?

Did you ever wonder why Elijah chose Mount Carmel as the place to confront the prophets of Baal and Asherah? Consider the following facts about Mount Carmel:

- It was more than 1,000 feet high and already had an altar (in bad repair) dedicated to God (1 Kings 18:30).
- It symbolized fertile splendor (Isaiah 35:1–2), typically receiving more than thirty inches of rain per year. (*Carmel* means "God's vineyard.")
- It was the most heavily forested area in Israel, making it an ideal place in which to show the Canaanites (who worshiped fertility gods) who really was the one true God.
- It was probably desolate after more than three years of drought, so the people knew that God, or perhaps Baal, was angry. This formerly lush site was a good illustration. (In other instances, Mount Carmel became withered as a result of curses. See Isaiah 33:9; Amos 1:2; and Nahum 1:4.)

**The Valley of Jezreel**

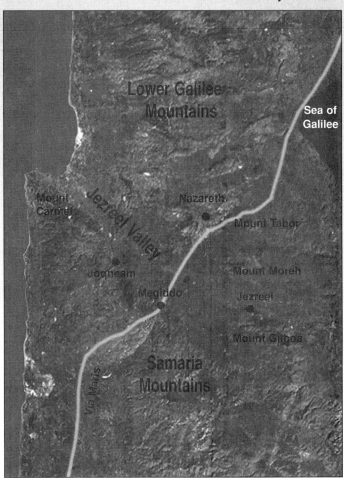

## WHY MOUNT CARMEL?

Did you ever wonder why Elijah chose Mount Carmel as the place to confront the prophets of Baal and Asherah? Consider the following facts about Mount Carmel:

- It was more than 1,000 feet high and already had an altar (in bad repair) dedicated to God (1 Kings 18:30).
- It symbolized fertile splendor (Isaiah 35:1–2), typically receiving more than thirty inches of rain per year. (*Carmel* means "God's vineyard.")
- It was the most heavily forested area in Israel, making it an ideal place in which to show the Canaanite (who worshiped fertility gods) who really was the one true God.
- It was probably desolate after more than three years of drought, so the people knew that God, or perhaps Baal, was angry. This formerly lush site was a good illustration. (In other instances, Mount Carmel became withered as a result of curses. See Isaiah 33:9; Amos 1:2; and Nahum 1:4.)

**The Valley of Jezreel**

## Small Group Bible Discovery (15 minutes)

> *Participant's Guide pages 53–64.*
>
> During this time, a group with fewer than seven participants will stay together. A group with seven or more participants will break into small groups and reassemble as a large group during the final five minutes. Assign each group one of the following topics. If you have more than five small groups, assign some topics to more than one group.

Let's break into groups of three to five—people sitting near you—and study some of the Bible passages and truths mentioned in the video.

Turn to pages 53–64 in your Participant's Guide. There you'll find a list of five topics. You'll have ten minutes to read and discuss the topic I'll assign to you. Choose one person in your group to be a spokesperson for your group when we discuss these topics later.

> Assign each group a topic.

I'll signal you when one minute is left.

## Topic A: Israel's Growing Confusion About God

✏ 1.   Shortly before his death, Joshua reviewed Israel's history, highlighting all that God had done for them. Then he asked the people of Israel to make a commitment to God. What was their response? (See Joshua 24:14–16, 22–25.)

*Suggested Response:* The people committed themselves to serve the Lord and to throw away all other gods.

✏ 2.   What does 1 Kings 11:6–11 reveal about Solomon's commitment to follow God and the consequences of his decision?

*Suggested Responses:* He did not keep his commitment to follow God, he built places of worship for other gods, he did evil in God's sight, God determined to divide the kingdom of Israel and take it away from Solomon because of Solomon's sin.

✏ 3.   What role did Jeroboam, the first king of the northern kingdom of Israel, play in leading the people away from God? (See 1 Kings 12:25–33.)

*Suggested Responses:* He set up two golden calves for the people to worship so they wouldn't have to worship God in Jerusalem. He presented those calves as the gods who brought them out of Egypt. He instituted feasts and a priesthood of his own making. By doing these things, he encouraged people to participate in the pagan worship of the Canaanites.

   a.   What was God's response? (See 1 Kings 13:1–3, 33–34.)

   *Suggested Response:* God sent a prophet to warn Jeroboam of the consequences of his evil ways, but he persisted in doing evil, so God destroyed the house of Jeroboam.

## small Group Bible Discovery

### Topic A: Israel's Growing Confusion About God

1. Shortly before his death, Joshua reviewed Israel's history, highlighting all that God had done for them. Then he asked the people of Israel to make a commitment to God. What was their response? (See Joshua 24:14–16, 22–25.)

2. What does 1 Kings 11:6–11 reveal about Solomon's commitment to follow God and the consequences of his decision?

3. What role did Jeroboam, the first king of the northern kingdom of Israel, play in leading the people away from God? (See 1 Kings 12:25–33.)

   a. What was God's response? (See 1 Kings 13:1–3, 33–34.)

b.  Look up the following verses and note Jeroboam's legacy among future kings of Israel.

| Reference | Legacy |
|---|---|
| 1 Kings 16:25–26 | Omri walked in the way of Jeroboam. |
| 2 Kings 10:31 | Jehu did not depart from the sins of Jeroboam. |
| 2 Kings 13:1–2 | Jehoahaz followed the sins of Jeroboam. |
| 2 Kings 13:10–11 | Jehoash walked in the sins of Jeroboam. |
| 2 Kings 14:23–24 | Jeroboam II did not depart from the sins of Jeroboam. |
| 2 Kings 15:8–9 | Zechariah did not depart from the sins of Jeroboam that made Israel sin. |
| 2 Kings 15:17–18 | Menahem did not depart from the sins of Jeroboam. |
| 2 Kings 15:23–24 | Pekahiah did not depart from the sins of Jeroboam. |
| 1 Kings 16:29–33 | Ahab walked in the sins of Jeroboam as if it were a trivial thing and did more to provoke the Lord than all the kings before him. |

4.  What impact did the kings' spiritual commitment have on the people of Israel? (See 1 Kings 18:17–21.)

*Suggested Response:* God sent Elijah to confront the Israelites concerning their commitment to follow God and God alone, but they wouldn't make their commitment known.

**THE TRUTH OF THE MATTER**

During Ahab's reign, he and the Israelites tried to serve both Yahweh and Baal. Unwilling to commit to one or the other, they worshiped both. They would honor Yahweh, then go to high places to sacrifice to Baal, burn incense under Asherah poles, and participate in religious rites with prostitutes. Elijah challenged them to consider their actions—to consider the futility of trying to serve two masters—and to make a choice. He knew that the values represented by Baal and God were contradictory.

Jesus also addressed the importance of choosing whom to serve when He commented on the futility of serving both God and money: "No one can serve two masters. Either he will hate the one and love the other, or he will be devoted to the one and despise the other" (Matthew 6:24).

54          Faith Lessons on the Prophets and Kings of Israel

b. Look up the following verses and note Jeroboam's legacy among future kings of Israel.

| Reference | Legacy |
|---|---|
| 1 Kings 16:25–26 | |
| 2 Kings 10:31 | |
| 2 Kings 13:1–2 | |
| 2 Kings 13:10–11 | |
| 2 Kings 14:23–24 | |
| 2 Kings 15:8–9 | |
| 2 Kings 15:17–18 | |
| 2 Kings 15:23–24 | |
| 1 Kings 16:29–33 | |

4. What impact did the kings' spiritual commitment have on the people of Israel? (See 1 Kings 18:17–21.)

---

Session Three: Who Is God?                                    55

### THE TRUTH OF THE MATTER

During Ahab's reign, he and the Israelites tried to serve both Yahweh and Baal. Unwilling to commit to one or the other, they worshiped both. They would honor Yahweh, then go to high places to sacrifice to Baal, burn incense under Asherah poles, and participate in religious rites with prostitutes. Elijah challenged them to consider their actions—to consider the futility of trying to serve two masters—and to make a choice. He knew that the values represented by Baal and God were contradictory.

Jesus also addressed the importance of choosing whom to serve when He commented on the futility of serving both God and money: "No one can serve two masters. Either he will hate the one and love the other, or he will be devoted to the one and despise the other" (Matthew 6:24).

### Topic B: The Role of God's Prophets

1. Through Moses, God promised that He would send prophets to help His people remain faithful to Him in a pagan world. These prophets would call people back to God's words and ways and communicate Yahweh's demand for total allegiance. Note what each of the following verses reveals about God's prophets.

a. Deuteronomy 18:14

b. Deuteronomy 18:15

c. Deuteronomy 18:18

## Topic B: The Role of God's Prophets

1.  Through Moses, God promised that He would send prophets to help His people remain faithful to Him in a pagan world. These prophets would call people back to God's words and ways and communicate Yahweh's demand for total allegiance. Note what each of the following verses reveals about God's prophets.

    a.  Deuteronomy 18:14

        *Suggested Response:* God recognized that the pagan cultures the Israelites would displace engaged in sinful, seductive practices such as sorcery and divination that He had commanded His people not to do.

    b.  Deuteronomy 18:15

        *Suggested Response:* God promised to raise up a prophet like Moses from among the Israelite people and commanded them to listen to him.

    c.  Deuteronomy 18:18

        *Suggested Response:* God would put His words into the prophet's mouth, and he would speak everything God would command him to speak.

    d.  Deuteronomy 18:19

        *Suggested Response:* Because God's prophet spoke on His behalf, God would hold the people responsible if they did not listen to him.

    e.  Deuteronomy 18:20

        *Suggested Response:* God held His prophets to a high standard of truth. A prophet who presumed to speak in God's name but really wasn't saying God's words, or who spoke in the name of other gods, would be put to death.

2.  What messages did God give to Elijah to give to Ahab? What was the purpose of those messages? How did Elijah know when to give them? (See 1 Kings 17:1–3; 18:1–2, 17–18.)

    *Suggested Responses:* God told Elijah to tell Ahab that it wouldn't rain; during the third year after that, God told him to go to Ahab and say that it would rain. Elijah said he was sent by God because Ahab had forsaken God's commandments and had worshiped Baal. Elijah knew what to do because "the word of the Lord came" to him.

3.  After God used Elijah to convict the Israelites of their sinfulness in worshiping Baal (1 Kings 18:39), one might think that Elijah would have had an easier life. But what happened soon afterward, and what does that reveal about the role of God's prophet? Read 1 Kings 19:1–4, 10.

    *Suggested Response:* When Queen Jezebel (Ahab's wife) learned how the 850 prophets of Baal and Asherah had been killed, she promised to kill Elijah. So Elijah ran away. In the desert, he sat under a tree and despaired for his life because Israel had forsaken God.

**THE TRUTH OF THE MATTER**

During Ahab's reign, he and the Israelites tried to serve both Yahweh and Baal. Unwilling to commit to one or the other, they worshiped both. They would honor Yahweh, then go to high places to sacrifice to Baal, burn incense under Asherah poles, and participate in religious rites with prostitutes. Elijah challenged them to consider their actions—to consider the futility of trying to serve two masters—and to make a choice. He knew that the values represented by Baal and God were contradictory.

Jesus also addressed the importance of choosing whom to serve when He commented on the futility of serving both God and money: "No one can serve two masters. Either he will hate the one and love the other, or he will be devoted to the one and despise the other" (Matthew 6:24).

**Topic B: The Role of God's Prophets**

1. Through Moses, God promised that He would send prophets to help His people remain faithful to Him in a pagan world. These prophets would call people back to God's words and ways and communicate Yahweh's demand for total allegiance. Note what each of the following verses reveals about God's prophets.

    a. Deuteronomy 18:14

    b. Deuteronomy 18:15

    c. Deuteronomy 18:18

    d. Deuteronomy 18:19

    e. Deuteronomy 18:20

**PROFILE OF FAITH**

**What Made Elijah Great?**

It's easy to think that Elijah was morally or spiritually superior to us, but he wasn't. He was just like us. He had strengths and weaknesses, good days and bad days. As the following Scriptures illustrate, he needed correction, encouragement, and the knowledge that other believers were standing against Baal, too.

- 1 Kings 19:3–4
  Fearing for his life, Elijah ran into the Negev Desert. Ready to quit, he prayed for death.
- 1 Kings 19:7–8
  God answered Elijah's prayer and provided food and drink.
- 1 Kings 19:10
  Elijah confessed his despair, fear, and weakness to God.
- 1 Kings 19:11–13
  After sending a powerful wind, earthquake, and fire, God revealed Himself to Elijah through a whisper.
- 1 Kings 19:18
  God revealed to lonely Elijah the encouraging news that 7,000 Israelites had not bowed their knees to Baal.

What made Elijah great? He completely committed himself to God and doing what God wanted him to do!

**PROFILE OF FAITH**

**What Made Elijah Great?**

It's easy to think that Elijah was morally or spiritually superior to us, but he wasn't. He was just like us. He had strengths and weaknesses, good days and bad days. As the following Scriptures illustrate, he needed correction, encouragement, and the knowledge that other believers were standing against Baal, too.

- 1 Kings 19:3–4
  Fearing for his life, Elijah ran into the Negev Desert. Ready to quit, he prayed for death.

- 1 Kings 19:7–8
  God answered Elijah's prayer and provided food and drink.

- 1 Kings 19:10
  Elijah confessed his despair, fear, and weakness to God.

- 1 Kings 19:11–13
  After sending a powerful wind, earthquake, and fire, God revealed Himself to Elijah through a whisper.

- 1 Kings 19:18
  God revealed to lonely Elijah the encouraging news that 7,000 Israelites had not bowed their knees to Baal.

What made Elijah great? He completely committed himself to God and doing what God wanted him to do!

## Topic C: The Significance of Biblical Names

In biblical times, people understood that a name expressed the essence or identity of a person. A good name thus meant more than even a good reputation because it identified the character of its bearer.

1. The word *Elijah* is composed of two Hebrew words: *El*, which means "god" and is a general reference to deity; and *Jah*, which is one part of the word *Yahweh* and represents the most holy name of God.

   a. Why is Elijah's name so significant in light of what he said to the Israelites in 1 Kings 18:21?

      *Suggested Response:* His name means "Yahweh is (my) God." So when he challenged the Israelites to choose which god they would serve, his choice was clear. In effect, his name answered the question, "Who is God?"

   b. How does what Elijah said in his prayer (1 Kings 18:36–37) relate to the meaning of his name?

      *Suggested Response:* Elijah asked God to answer his prayer so that the people would know the meaning of his name—that Yahweh was God.

d. Deuteronomy 18:19

e. Deuteronomy 18:20

### PROFILE OF FAITH

**What Made Elijah Great?**

It's easy to think that Elijah was morally or spiritually superior to us, but he wasn't. He was just like us. He had strengths and weaknesses, good days and bad days. As the following Scriptures illustrate, he needed correction, encouragement, and the knowledge that other believers were standing against Baal, too.

- 1 Kings 19:3–4
  Fearing for his life, Elijah ran into the Negev Desert. Ready to quit, he prayed for death.
- 1 Kings 19:7–8
  God answered Elijah's prayer and provided food and drink.
- 1 Kings 19:10
  Elijah confessed his despair, fear, and weakness to God.
- 1 Kings 19:11–13
  After sending a powerful wind, earthquake, and fire, God revealed Himself to Elijah through a whisper.
- 1 Kings 19:18
  God revealed to lonely Elijah the encouraging news that 7,000 Israelites had not bowed their knees to Baal.

What made Elijah great? He completely committed himself to God and doing what God wanted him to do!

2. What messages did God give to Elijah to give to Ahab? What was the purpose of those messages? How did Elijah know when to give them? (See 1 Kings 17:1–3; 18:1–2, 17–18.)

3. After God used Elijah to convict the Israelites of their sinfulness in worshiping Baal (1 Kings 18:39), one might think that Elijah would have had an easier life. But what happened soon afterward, and what does that reveal about the role of God's prophet? Read 1 Kings 19:1–4, 10.

**Topic C: The Significance of Biblical Names**

In biblical times, people understood that a name expressed the essence or identity of a person. A good name thus meant more than even a good reputation because it identified the character of its bearer.

1. The word *Elijah* is composed of two Hebrew words: *El*, which means "god," and is a general reference to deity; *Jah*, which is one part of the word *Yahweh* and represents the most holy name of God.

   a. Why is Elijah's name so significant in light of what he said to the Israelites in 1 Kings 18:21?

   b. How does what Elijah said in his prayer (1 Kings 18:36–37) relate to the meaning of his name?

**PLANNING NOTES:**

✎ 2. What did God demonstrate when He changed Abram's name to Abraham (Genesis 17:1–5)? What did Pharaoh demonstrate when he renamed Joseph (Genesis 41:45)?

*Suggested Responses:* God demonstrated His authority over Abraham; Pharaoh demonstrated his authority over Joseph.

✎ 3. In the Near East, a person's name identified something about the person's character or circumstances (such as birth or family).

a. Why did Sarah and Abraham name their son "Isaac," which means "he laughs"? (See Genesis 17:17.)

*Suggested Response:* When God told 100-year-old Abraham that his 90-year-old wife would give birth, he laughed.

b. Why did Moses receive his name, which meant "to draw out"? (See Exodus 2:1–10.)

*Suggested Response:* Because the infant Moses was pulled from the Nile River, where he was found floating in a basket.

✎ 4. In Matthew 1:20–21, we read that an angel told Joseph in a dream that his wife Mary would give birth to a son, and that he was to give the baby a specific name. What was this name, and why was it given?

*Suggested Response:* The name was Jesus, and it was given because He would save His people from their sins. Jesus is a shortened version of "Yehoshua" or "Joshua," which means "Yahweh saves."

✎ 5. When God told Moses, "I know you by name" (Exodus 33:17), what was He saying besides the fact that He recognizes us as individuals?

*Suggested Response:* God is saying that He completely understands who and what we are.

## Topic D: "High Places"

✎ 1. God allowed His people to employ cultural practices and ideas if they had no pagan content and were used only in God's service. Since the people of the ancient Near East honored their gods by worshiping them on high places, God allowed His people to build altars to Him—and Him alone—on high places. He also communicated with His people on high places. The following verses will help you gain a picture of the appropriate use of high places.

| Reference | High Place Events |
|---|---|
| Genesis 22:1–2, 9–14 | God told Abraham to sacrifice his beloved son on top of a mountain. In faith, Abraham was prepared to do that, but God intervened and provided a ram for the sacrifice. |
| Exodus 19:20–22; 31:18 | God called Moses to the top of Mount Sinai, where they spoke together and where Moses received the Ten Commandments. |

(continued on page 98)

2. What did God demonstrate when He changed Abram's name to Abraham (Genesis 17:1–5)? What did Pharaoh demonstrate when he renamed Joseph (Genesis 41:45)?

3. In the Near East, a person's name identified something about the person's character or circumstances (such as birth or family).

   a. Why did Sarah and Abraham name their son "Isaac," which means "he laughs"? (See Genesis 17:17.)

   b. Why did Moses receive his name, which meant "to draw out"? (See Exodus 2:1–10.)

4. In Matthew 1:20–21, we read that an angel told Joseph in a dream that his wife Mary would give birth to a son, and that he was to give the baby a specific name. What was this name, and why was it given?

5. When God told Moses, "I know you by name" (Exodus 33:17), what was He saying besides the fact that He recognizes us as individuals?

**Topic D: "High Places"**

1. God allowed His people to employ cultural practices and ideas if they had no pagan content and were used only in God's service. Since the people of the ancient Near East honored their gods by worshiping them on high places, God allowed His people to build altars to Him—and Him alone—on high places. He also communicated with His people on high places. The following verses will help you gain a picture of the appropriate use of high places.

| Reference | High Place Events |
|---|---|
| Genesis 22:1–2, 9–14 | |
| Exodus 19:20–22; 31:18 | |
| Numbers 22:41; 23:1–5 | |
| Deuteronomy 27:1–7; Joshua 8:30–31 | |
| Judges 6:25–27 | |

(continued on page 60)

(continued from page 96)

| Reference | High Place Events |
|---|---|
| Numbers 22:41; 23:1–5 | After sacrificing to God on a high place of Baal, Balaam the prophet went to a "barren height" where God spoke to him. |
| Deuteronomy 27:1–7; Joshua 8:30–31 | After they crossed the Jordan River into Canaan, the people of Israel were to set up plaster-coated stones on top of Mount Ebal and build a stone altar and offer burnt offerings to God. Joshua fulfilled this task years later when he renewed the Israelites' covenant with God. |
| Judges 6:25–27 | Gideon broke down the altar to Baal that his father had built on a high place and cut down the Asherah pole. Then he built an altar to God at the very top of the high place and offered a bull as a burnt offering. |
| 1 Samuel 9:10–14 | When Saul and his servant asked where they would find Samuel, they were told that he would soon be going up to a high place to bless a sacrifice for the people. |
| 1 Chronicles 21:18–26 | In response to God's command, David built an altar to the Lord on the threshing floor of Araunah the Jebusite, which was on Mount Moriah. |
| 2 Chronicles 3:1 | Solomon built God's temple on Mount Moriah, on the same site where David, his father, had built an altar to the Lord. |

**The Temple Mount at Jerusalem**

2. What did God tell the Israelites to do with the high places where the Canaanites worshiped? (See Deuteronomy 7:5; Numbers 33:52.)

*Suggested Responses:* To destroy the carved and cast idols of Canaan's inhabitants, break down pagan altars, smash the pagans' sacred stones, cut down their Asherah poles, and demolish all the pagan high places so God's people would not be tempted to blend worship of false gods with the worship of Yahweh, the one true God.

5. When God told Moses, "I know you by name" (Exodus 33:17), what was He saying besides the fact that He recognizes us as individuals?

**Topic D: "High Places"**

1. God allowed His people to employ cultural practices and ideas if they had no pagan content and were used only in God's service. Since the people of the ancient Near East honored their gods by worshiping them on high places, God allowed His people to build altars to Him—and Him alone—on high places. He also communicated with His people on high places. The following verses will help you gain a picture of the appropriate use of high places.

| Reference | High Place Events |
|---|---|
| Genesis 22:1–2, 9–14 | |
| Exodus 19:20–22; 31:18 | |
| Numbers 22:41; 23:1–5 | |
| Deuteronomy 27:1–7; Joshua 8:30–31 | |
| Judges 6:25–27 | |

(continued on page 60)

(continued from page 59)

| Reference | High Place Events |
|---|---|
| 1 Samuel 9:10–14 | |
| 1 Chronicles 21:18–26 | |
| 2 Chronicles 3:1 | |

**The Temple Mount at Jerusalem**

2. What did God tell the Israelites to do with the high places where the Canaanites worshiped? (See Deuteronomy 7:5; Numbers 33:52.)

✏ **3.** The Israelites didn't follow God's commands concerning high places. What, in fact, did the Israelites do in the high places and what was the result? (See 2 Kings 17:6–12.)

*Suggested Responses:* The Israelites sinned against the Lord by building high places in all their towns, worshiping other gods, and following pagan practices. As a result, the Israelites in Samaria were deported to Assyria.

**The Altar at Megiddo**

## DATA FILE

### The High Place and Altar at Dan

When Israel was divided into the northern kingdom (Israel) and the southern kingdom (Judah) in 920 B.C., the high place at Dan was established as a worship site in northern Israel. Archaeological evidence indicates that it:

- Measured sixty-two feet square.
- Was surrounded by a wall, with a staircase leading up to it.
- Had buildings on it that housed the shrine or "idol" that was worshiped there.

Three different high places were built on the same site.

#### Site 1

This site dates to King Jeroboam in the tenth century B.C., who—after Israel split into two parts—needed an alternative to the temple established by David and Solomon in Jerusalem. Jeroboam worshiped a golden calf on this site (1 Kings 12:26–30), which had a platform sixty feet long and twenty feet wide and an altar in front of the steps. Avraham Biran, the archaeologist directing this excavation, discovered that the fire that destroyed the shrine of Jeroboam had also turned the stones red.

#### Site 2

Someone, probably King Ahab, rebuilt the high place and made it larger. The Israelites continued to sink deeper into pagan practices and values.

(continued on page 102)

3. The Israelites didn't follow God's commands concerning high places. What, in fact, did the Israelites do in the high places and what was the result? (See 2 Kings 17:6–12.)

The Altar at Megiddo

**DATA FILE**

**The High Place and Altar at Dan**
When Israel was divided into the northern kingdom (Israel) and the southern kingdom (Judah) in 920 B.C., the high place at Dan was established as a worship site in northern Israel. Archaeological evidence indicates that it:
- Measured sixty-two feet square.
- Was surrounded by a wall, with a staircase leading up to it.
- Had buildings on it that housed the shrine or "idol" that was worshiped there.

Three different high places were built on the same site.

(continued on page 62)

---

(continued from page 61)
*Site 1*
This site dates to King Jeroboam in the tenth century B.C., who—after Israel split into two parts—needed an alternative to the temple established by David and Solomon in Jerusalem. Jeroboam worshiped a golden calf on this site (1 Kings 12:26–30), which had a platform sixty feet long and twenty feet wide and an altar in front of the steps. Avraham Biran, the archaeologist directing this excavation, discovered that the fire that destroyed the shrine of Jeroboam had also turned the stones red.

*Site 2*
Someone, probably King Ahab, rebuilt the high place and made it larger. The Israelites continued to sink deeper into pagan practices and values.

*Site 3*
During the reign of Jeroboam II (ca. 760 B.C.), a large staircase and altar in front of this massive high place were added. Only parts of this altar, such as one of the horns that protruded from the four corners and part of the stairs leading to the altar, have been found.

During Jeroboam's reign, the prophet Amos predicted the final destruction of Israel because of its idolatry and pagan practices (Amos 3:12–15; 5:11–15; 8:14). Thirty years later, the brutal Assyrian army destroyed the northern ten tribes, who ceased to exist. Ashes and burn marks from a great fire on the altar and high place confirm Amos' prediction.

The High Place and Altar at Dan

(continued from page 100)

### Site 3

During the reign of Jeroboam II (ca. 760 B.C.), a large staircase and altar in front of this massive high place were added. Only parts of this altar, such as one of the horns that protruded from the four corners and part of the stairs leading to the altar, have been found.

During Jeroboam's reign, the prophet Amos predicted the final destruction of Israel because of its idolatry and pagan practices (Amos 3:12–15; 5:11–15; 8:14). Thirty years later, the brutal Assyrian army destroyed the northern ten tribes, who ceased to exist. Ashes and burn marks from a great fire on the altar and high place confirm Amos' prediction.

**The High Place and Altar at Dan**

## Topic E: Ways in Which God Reveals That He Is God

1. What does God use in our world today to reveal that He is God? (See Isaiah 43:11–12.)

   *Suggested Responses:* God uses ordinary people who have put their faith and trust in Him and His salvation and are committed to worship Him and Him alone.

2. How did God prove Himself to Pharaoh? (See Exodus 7:17, 20.)

   *Suggested Response:* Moses struck the water of the Nile with his staff, and the water turned into blood.

3. How did God prove Himself and His mighty power to "all the peoples of the earth"? (See Joshua 4:21–24.)

   *Suggested Response:* God dried up the Jordan River, just as He had dried up the Red Sea, so that the Israelites could cross.

62          Faith Lessons on the Prophets and Kings of Israel

(continued from page 61)

### Site 1

This site dates to King Jeroboam in the tenth century B.C., who—after Israel split into two parts—needed an alternative to the temple established by David and Solomon in Jerusalem. Jeroboam worshiped a golden calf on this site (1 Kings 12:26–30), which had a platform sixty feet long and twenty feet wide and an altar in front of the steps. Avraham Biran, the archaeologist directing this excavation, discovered that the fire that destroyed the shrine of Jeroboam had also turned the stones red.

### Site 2

Someone, probably King Ahab, rebuilt the high place and made it larger. The Israelites continued to sink deeper into pagan practices and values.

### Site 3

During the reign of Jeroboam II (ca. 760 B.C.), a large staircase and altar in front of this massive high place were added. Only parts of this altar, such as one of the horns that protruded from the four corners and part of the stairs leading to the altar, have been found.

During Jeroboam's reign, the prophet Amos predicted the final destruction of Israel because of its idolatry and pagan practices (Amos 3:12–15; 5:11–15; 8:14). Thirty years later, the brutal Assyrian army destroyed the northern ten tribes, who ceased to exist. Ashes and burn marks from a great fire on the altar and high place confirm Amos' prediction.

**The High Place and Altar at Dan**

---

Session Three: Who Is God?                                          63

## Topic E: Ways in Which God Reveals That He Is God

1. What does God use in our world today to reveal that He is God? (See Isaiah 43:11–12.)

2. How did God prove Himself to Pharaoh? (See Exodus 7:17, 20.)

3. How did God prove Himself and His mighty power to "all the peoples of the earth"? (See Joshua 4:21–24.)

4. What did Solomon say in front of the entire assembly of Israel? (See 1 Kings 8:59–60.)

5. Why did David fight Goliath? (See 1 Samuel 17:45–47.)

✏ 4.   What did Solomon say in front of the entire assembly of Israel? (See 1 Kings 8:59–60.)

*Suggested Response:* He wanted the words he had prayed to motivate God to uphold the cause of the Israelites so that all people would know that "the LORD is God and that there is no other."

✏ 5.   Why did David fight Goliath? (See 1 Samuel 17:45–47.)

*Suggested Response:* So that everyone would know that there was a God in Israel.

✏ 6.   What had God done to demonstrate Himself to the Canaanites, including Rahab, the prostitute who lived in Jericho? What was the effect? (See Joshua 2:8–11.)

*Suggested Responses:* God led His people out of Egypt, across the Red Sea, and enabled the Israelites to completely destroy the two kings of the Amorites. The people of Jericho lost their courage because the Israelites' God was the God of heaven and earth.

✏ 7.   What did Hezekiah pray after being challenged by the powerful Assyrian king? (See Isaiah 37:18–20.)

*Suggested Response:* Hezekiah prayed that God would deliver His people so that every kingdom on earth would know that God, and God alone, was God.

✏ 8.   What did God do for Namaan to cause him to bless God? And what did Namaan affirm afterward? (See 2 Kings 5:13–15.)

*Suggested Responses:* God healed Namaan of his leprosy. Namaan recognized that there was "no God in all the world except in Israel."

> After nine minutes, let participants know that they have one minute remaining. Then reassemble the entire group. After everyone is back together, begin asking one person from each small group to briefly share a key idea with the larger group. In some cases, you may not have time for every group to share their discoveries.

As time allows, let's briefly share the key ideas that your group discussed.

**Topic E: Ways in Which God Reveals That He Is God**

1.  What does God use in our world today to reveal that He is God? (See Isaiah 43:11–12.)

2.  How did God prove Himself to Pharaoh? (See Exodus 7:17, 20.)

3.  How did God prove Himself and His mighty power to "all the peoples of the earth"? (See Joshua 4:21–24.)

4.  What did Solomon say in front of the entire assembly of Israel? (See 1 Kings 8:59–60.)

5.  Why did David fight Goliath? (See 1 Samuel 17:45–47.)

6.  What had God done to demonstrate Himself to the Canaanites, including Rahab, the prostitute who lived in Jericho? What was the effect? (See Joshua 2:8–11.)

7.  What did Hezekiah pray after being challenged by the powerful Assyrian king? (See Isaiah 37:18–20.)

8.  What did God do for Namaan to cause him to bless God? And what did Namaan affirm afterward? (See 2 Kings 5:13–15.)

**PLANNING NOTES:**

# fɑith Lesson

**Time for Reflection (4 minutes)**

On page 65 of your Participant's Guide, you'll find a passage of Scripture. Let's each read this passage silently and take the next few minutes to consider some of the questions that follow the Scripture passage.

Please do not talk during this time. It's a time when we all can consider who is Lord of our lives.

> *The Scripture passage and questions are reproduced in their entirety in the Participant's Guide on pages 65–66.*

Then Elijah said to all the people, "Come here to me." They came to him, and he repaired the altar of the LORD, which was in ruins. Elijah took twelve stones, one for each of the tribes descended from Jacob, to whom the word of the LORD had come, saying, "Your name shall be Israel." With the stones he built an altar in the name of the LORD, and he dug a trench around it large enough to hold two seahs of seed. He arranged the wood, cut the bull into pieces and laid it on the wood. Then he said to them, "Fill four large jars with water and pour it on the offering and on the wood." "Do it again," he said, and they did it again. "Do it a third time," he ordered, and they did it the third time. The water ran down around the altar and even filled the trench. At the time of sacrifice, the prophet Elijah stepped forward and prayed: "O LORD, God of Abraham, Isaac and Israel, let it be known today that you are God in Israel and that I am your servant and have done all these things at your command. Answer me, O LORD, answer me, so these people will know that you, O LORD, are God, and that you are turning their hearts back again." Then the fire of the LORD fell and burned up the sacrifice, the wood, the stones and the soil, and also licked up the water in the trench. When all the people saw this, they fell prostrate and cried, "The LORD—he is God! The LORD—he is God!" Then Elijah commanded them, "Seize the prophets of Baal. Don't let anyone get away!" They seized them, and Elijah had them brought down to the Kishon Valley and slaughtered there.... Now Ahab told Jezebel everything Elijah had done and how he had killed all the prophets with the sword. So Jezebel sent a messenger to Elijah to say, "May the gods deal with me, be it ever so severely, if by this time tomorrow I do not make your life like that of one of them." Elijah was afraid and ran for his life.

1 KINGS 18:30–40; 19:1–3A

✏ 1.   Just as Elijah's very identity was a testimony to his commitment to God, your identity can be built on God. How can you, in God's power, reveal the person and presence of God to other people?

✏ 2.   What are the most significant "Baals" (evils) that lure people away from God in your culture today?

# faith Lesson

## Time for Reflection

Read the following passage of Scripture and take the next few minutes to consider who is Lord of your life.

> Then Elijah said to all the people, "Come here to me." They came to him, and he repaired the altar of the LORD, which was in ruins. Elijah took twelve stones, one for each of the tribes descended from Jacob, to whom the word of the LORD had come, saying, "Your name shall be Israel." With the stones he built an altar in the name of the LORD, and he dug a trench around it large enough to hold two seahs of seed. He arranged the wood, cut the bull into pieces and laid it on the wood. Then he said to them, "Fill four large jars with water and pour it on the offering and on the wood." "Do it again," he said, and they did it again. "Do it a third time," he ordered, and they did it the third time. The water ran down around the altar and even filled the trench. At the time of sacrifice, the prophet Elijah stepped forward and prayed: "O LORD, God of Abraham, Isaac and Israel, let it be known today that you are God in Israel and that I am your servant and have done all these things at your command. Answer me, O LORD, answer me, so these people will know that you, O LORD, are God, and that you are turning their hearts back again." Then the fire of the LORD fell and burned up the sacrifice, the wood, the stones and the soil, and also licked up the water in the trench. When all the people saw this, they fell prostrate and cried, "The LORD—he is God! The LORD—he is God!" Then Elijah commanded them, "Seize the prophets of Baal. Don't let anyone get away!" They seized them, and Elijah had them brought down to the Kishon Valley and slaughtered there.... Now Ahab told Jezebel everything Elijah had done and how he had killed all the prophets with the sword. So Jezebel sent a messenger to Elijah to say, "May the gods deal with me, be it ever so severely, if by this time tomorrow I do not make your life like that of one of them." Elijah was afraid and ran for his life.

> 1 KINGS 18:30–40; 19:1–3A

1. Just as Elijah's very identity was a testimony to his commitment to God, your identity can be built on God. How can you, in God's power, reveal the person and presence of God to other people?

2. What are the most significant "Baals" (evils) that lure people away from God in your culture today?

3. Which method(s) are most effective in bringing the power of God to bear against these evils?

4. What would God have you do—given your time, resources, opportunities—to call your culture to faith in God and lead others to godly obedience?

5. What might be the price of your commitment to reveal God to your culture?

✏ 3.  Which method(s) are most effective in bringing the power of God to bear against these evils?

✏ 4.  What would God have you do—given your time, resources, opportunities—to call your culture to faith in God and lead others to godly obedience?

✏ 5.  What might be the price of your commitment to reveal God to your culture?

## Action Points (3 minutes)

> *The following points are reproduced on pages 67–68 of the Participant's Guide:*

Now it's time to wrap up our session.

> **Give participants a moment to transition from their thoughtfulness to giving you their full attention.**

I'd like to take a moment to summarize the key points we explored. After I have reviewed these points, I will give you a moment to jot down an action step (or steps) that you will commit to this week as a result of what you have learned today.

> **Read the following points and pause after each so that participants can consider and write out their commitments.**

✏ 1.  *God demands that we recognize that He alone is Lord of our lives. He calls us to follow Him obediently and not to waver. We are to serve Him wholeheartedly and not to trust in other gods.*

When Elijah challenged the Israelites to stop wavering between God and Baal, they were silent. Indeed, they didn't stand up for God until after He sent fire down from heaven that burned up Elijah's sacrifice and the altar on which it stood. In contrast, when Joshua challenged the Israelites years earlier to evaluate whom they would serve (Joshua 24:15), they resoundingly said that they would serve the Lord.

**In what ways do you waver between serving God completely and placing faith in something or someone else?**

✏ 2.  *When we live out who God has made us to be, people will see God.*

Elijah, whose very name meant "Yahweh is God," did what God called him to do, and the people saw the evidence of God in a powerful way. When the Israelites recognized who God was, they renounced Baal and killed the prophets of Baal and Asherah.

**As people observe you in daily life—at home, at work, at play—what do they see? Do they see someone who is totally committed to God and following His ways? When they see you, are they reminded of who God is ... whether or not they choose to follow Him?**

1. Just as Elijah's very identity was a testimony to his commitment to God, your identity can be built on God. How can you, in God's power, reveal the person and presence of God to other people?

2. What are the most significant "Baals" (evils) that lure people away from God in your culture today?

3. Which method(s) are most effective in bringing the power of God to bear against these evils?

4. What would God have you do—given your time, resources, opportunities—to call your culture to faith in God and lead others to godly obedience?

5. What might be the price of your commitment to reveal God to your culture?

**Action Points**

Take a few minutes to review the key points you explored today, then write down an action step (or steps) that you will commit to this week as a result of what you have learned.

1. *God demands that we recognize that He alone is Lord of our lives. He calls us to follow Him obediently and not to waver. We are to serve Him wholeheartedly and not to trust in other gods.*

   When Elijah challenged the Israelites to stop wavering between God and Baal, they were silent. Indeed, they didn't stand up for God until after He sent fire down from heaven that burned up Elijah's sacrifice and the altar on which it stood. In contrast, when Joshua challenged the Israelites years earlier to evaluate whom they would serve (Joshua 24:15), they resoundingly said that they would serve the Lord.

   **In what ways do you waver between serving God completely and placing faith in something or someone else?**

2. *When we live out who God has made us to be, people will see God.*

   Elijah, whose very name meant "Yahweh is God," did what God called him to do, and the people saw the evidence of God in a powerful way. When the Israelites recognized who God was, they renounced Baal and killed the prophets of Baal and Asherah.

   **As people observe you in daily life—at home, at work, at play—what do they see? Do they see someone who is totally committed to God and following His ways? When**

What commitment are you willing to make to becoming a modern "Elijah," a living witness of God's power and presence who passionately reflects God in everything you do?

# closing prayer

1 minute

This lesson has challenged us to examine our commitment to God and realize that He can use us to show others who He really is. Let's close in prayer now, asking God to give us the courage to fulfill the calling He has given us and to allow us to reflect His character to other people who desperately need to know Him.

*Dear God, when the Israelites wavered in their faith between the gods of their culture and You, You sent Elijah—a person like us—to remind them of who You are. Thank You for loving us enough to send Jesus to earth to die on the cross and rise again, and for giving us the Holy Spirit to guide and comfort us. Help us to stand up for You and Your values in our everyday world, to reflect You in all that we do, say, and think. We want people to see You living through us, Lord. Please help us to be strong, living testimonies to who You are—the one true God, Yahweh. Amen.*

they see you, are they reminded of who God is . . . whether or not they choose to follow Him?

What commitment are you willing to make to becoming a modern "Elijah," a living witness of God's power and presence who passionately reflects God in everything you do?

# The wages of sin

## Before you lead

### Synopsis

The ruins of Lachish stand as a monument to what can happen when a culture refuses to follow God's ways and violates the standards revealed in His Word. Once one of ancient Israel's largest cities, Lachish defended Israel's southern flank, protecting Jerusalem from invaders that might come up from Egypt. As you view the ruins of the city's massive gate, which is the largest gate structure found in Israel, the city's amazing strength and its importance become evident. You can almost picture crowds of people walking along the cobblestone streets and conducting business in the compartments of the inner gate.

To understand what happened at Lachish, you must go back to about 920 B.C., when Israel split into two parts: the northern ten tribes becoming the nation called Israel and the southern tribes becoming the kingdom of Judah. As we learn from 2 Kings 17, the people of Israel and Judah chose not to follow their God and did "wicked things that provoked the LORD to anger." They worried about prosperity and personal success instead of faithfulness and obedience to God. Caught up in the seductive religion of their culture, they repeatedly sought pagan answers and worshiped idols, although the Lord had said, "You shall not do this" (2 Kings 17:12).

In response, God sent prophets and seers to turn His people back to Him. But after generations of warnings, the Israelites still refused to follow God and listen to His prophets. When His patience was finally exhausted, God allowed foreign nations to invade the land and punish His people.

In 722 B.C., God allowed the cruel Assyrians (from the area we know as Iraq) to utterly destroy the ten northern tribes of Israel. Then the Assyrians turned their sights on Lachish, the gateway to Jerusalem. During the siege and fall of Lachish, as many as 50,000 people were brutally tortured and killed. Even those who faithfully had followed God died. The few prisoners who were taken to Assyria were led along by rings pierced through their lips.

The king of Assyria, Sennacherib, then captured all the fortified cities of Judah and marched his huge army to Jerusalem, where Hezekiah (king of Judah) reigned. But all was not lost. Hezekiah was unlike many of his predecessors. Instead of promoting idol worship, Hezekiah had followed God's standards. He had tried valiantly to impact his culture for God. In an effort to end the moral decay of his culture, Hezekiah had removed high places, smashed sacred stones, cut down Asherah poles, and destroyed idols. And, in preparation for enemy attack, he commissioned the digging of a water tunnel more than 1,500 feet long that would provide water for Jerusalem during an extended siege.

Sennacherib, however, had no regard for the God of Israel and taunted Hezekiah. "How can you depend on your God?" he asked, in effect. "I'm going to make you suffer just as I've made everybody else suffer. Your God can't deliver you. You are finished."

Hezekiah, however, had been raised up at that particular time to meet a particular need—to do what God intended him to do, to keep God's plan of salvation going. So he laid the threatening letter from Sennacherib before God in the temple and prayed that God would deliver His people so that "all kingdoms on earth may know that you alone, O Lord, are God" (2 Kings 19:19).

God heard that prayer. He had seen Hezekiah's commitment to Him and promised to defend Jerusalem. That night, the angel of the Lord killed 185,000 Assyrian soldiers, and Sennacherib returned to Assyria without attacking Jerusalem.

Ray Vander Laan points out that we stand in a similar place today. Because of the immorality and evils of our culture, God's judgment hangs over us as well. He waits for those who are totally devoted to Him to stand up and impact their culture, to accomplish His purposes and turn the hearts of the people back toward God.

## Key Points of This Lesson

1. *When a culture fails to live out its God-given calling and disobeys the standards found in His Word, God may send judgment on the entire culture—those who are godly as well as those who persist in wrongdoing.*

    For generations, Israel and Judah disobeyed God repeatedly even though He kept calling them back to Himself. They persisted in idol worship and refused to commit themselves to Him and to the lifestyle He requires. So God finally sent judgment in the form of the Assyrian army.

2. *It is God's desire that those who love Him make an impact on their culture.* Those who are wholly devoted to God and are willing to stand against evil can be very effective in redeeming the culture.

    Because of Hezekiah's faithful devotion to God, he was able to impact his culture in godly ways and ultimately helped to bring about God's purposes in the world—Jesus' lineage through the tribe of Judah. At the heart of his effectiveness was the fact that Hezekiah did what was right, prepared for the difficulties to come while trusting God completely, and truly desired that the world would know that God is God.

## Session Outline (55 minutes)

    **I. Introduction** (3 minutes)
    Welcome
    What's to Come
    Questions to Think About

    **II. Show Video "The Wages of Sin"** (23 minutes)

    **III. Group Discovery** (20 minutes)
    Video Highlights
    Small Group Bible Discovery

    **IV. Faith Lesson** (8 minutes)
    Time for Reflection
    Action Points

    **V. Closing Prayer** (1 minute)

## Materials

No additional materials are needed for this session. Simply view the video prior to leading the session so you are familiar with its main points.

# The wages of sin

## introduction

3 minutes

### Welcome

Assemble the participants together. Welcome them to session four of *Faith Lessons on the Prophets and Kings of Israel.*

### What's to Come

God commanded the Israelites to follow Him and to obey Him, which included not worshiping other gods. But the Israelites didn't listen to God, nor to the prophets He sent to warn them. So God allowed other nations to punish His people. About 740 B.C., the Assyrians utterly destroyed the ten tribes of Israel, then moved into Judah and destroyed the city of Lachish where much of this session was filmed. But Hezekiah, king of Judah, had obeyed and trusted God, so He miraculously delivered Jerusalem from Assyria.

In this session, Ray Vander Laan highlights that any culture—including ours—will eventually face God's judgment if it refuses to follow His ways. Ray strongly encourages all Christians to actively influence their culture for God. He points out that Christians who desire to obey God don't have the option of not impacting culture.

### Questions to Think About

*Participant's Guide page 69.*

Ask each question and solicit a few responses from group members.

1. If you suddenly learned that God would send His judgment upon your culture—including the people who are following Him—within two years unless people turn back to Him, how would you live differently this week?

   *Suggested Responses:* may include telling more people at work and in my neighborhood about Jesus, becoming more involved in the media so that God's truths could be heard by more people, working harder at obeying God, spending more time getting to know God instead of being so busy with other things, etc.

2. Which aspects of your culture do you think are most displeasing to God? Why are they an affront to Him?

   *Suggested Responses:* may include the worship of false gods such as fame, money, and relationships; pride that takes credit for what God is doing; the

---

**SESSION FOUR**

## The wages of sin

### questions to think about

1. If you suddenly learned that God would send His judgment upon your culture—including the people who are following Him—within two years unless people turn back to Him, how would you live differently this week?

2. Which aspects of your culture do you think are most displeasing to God? Why are they an affront to Him?

69

---

increasing tendency to disobey God's Word; the unwillingness to call sin sin; the rise of New Age activities, homosexual agendas, and deceit; the fact that for most people morality is subjective; etc.

Let's keep these ideas in mind as we view the video.

# video presentation

**23** minutes          *Participant's Guide page 70.*

On page 70 of your Participant's Guide, you will find a space in which to take notes on key points as we watch this video.

## Leader's Video Observations

Lachish—a Great City, a Terrible Fall

God's Judgment at the Hand of the Assyrians

Hezekiah's Example

Our Mandate to Impact Culture

## video notes

**Lachish—a Great City, a Terrible Fall**

**God's Judgment at the Hand of the Assyrians**

**Hezekiah's Example**

**Our Mandate to Impact Culture**

# Group Discovery

**20** minutes

If your group has seven or more members, use the **Video Highlights** with the entire group (5 minutes), then break into small groups of three to five to discuss the **Small Group Bible Discovery** (10 minutes). Then reassemble the group to discuss the key points discovered (5 minutes).

If your group has fewer than seven members, begin with the **Video Highlights** (5 minutes), then do one or more of the topics found in the **Small Group Bible Discovery** as a group (10 minutes). Finally, spend five minutes at the end discussing points that had an impact on participants.

## Video Highlights (5 minutes)

Here you'll ask one or more of the following questions that directly relate to the video the participants have just seen.

1. What did you learn through this video about the nature of the ongoing battle between good and evil?

   *Suggested Responses:* Allow participants to share their views. Help them to grasp the reality of the fierce battle at Lachish, where very righteous people lived (and suffered) among the unrighteous; that the battle really is the Lord's; that one righteous person can make a difference in the culture; that God's tolerance of evil has a limit, and He will send His judgment upon an unrepentant, evil culture; that wholehearted devotion to God is essential to making a godly impact on culture; etc.

2. Why did God allow the Assyrians to annihilate the ten tribes of Israel?

   *Suggested Response:* After giving His people many opportunities to repent and follow His ways again, God finally could tolerate their hardened and disobedient hearts no longer.

3. What did King Hezekiah do when challenged by the Assyrian king?

   *Suggested Responses:* humbled himself before God, praised God, sought God's help even though he had already prepared for attack, asked God to act so that people would remember that He alone is God, etc.

4. Certainly many other righteous people before him had prayed to God for deliverance from the Assyrians, so why do you think God responded as He did to Hezekiah's prayer?

   *Suggested Responses:* will vary, but may include that Hezekiah had clearly demonstrated his commitment to follow God by destroying the false gods and places of idol worship; he wanted people to know that God alone is God; God preserved a remnant of His people in order to carry out His plans for them and the world as a whole; etc.

# video highlights

1. What did you learn through this video about the nature of the ongoing battle between good and evil?

2. Why did God allow the Assyrians to annihilate the ten tribes of Israel?

3. What did King Hezekiah do when challenged by the Assyrian king?

4. Certainly many other righteous people before him had prayed to God for deliverance from the Assyrians, so why do you think God responded as He did to Hezekiah's prayer?

**PLANNING NOTES:**

## THE TRUTH OF THE MATTER

### The Terrible Assyrians

Their empire was located in Mesopotamia near the Euphrates River.

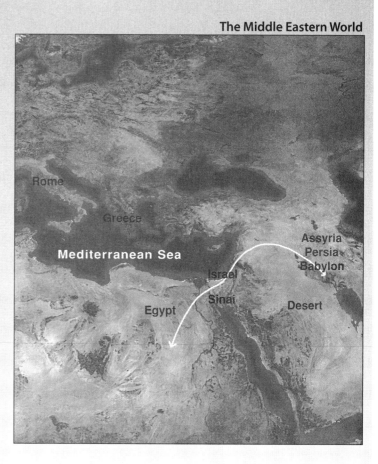

**The Middle Eastern World**

The people had such a bad reputation that Jonah fled when God commanded him to speak to Nineveh, Assyria's capital (Jonah 1:1–3).

Known for their ruthlessness in battle and horrific treatment of captives, Assyrian soldiers were equipped with the latest weaponry—barbed arrows, catapults, and siege machines.

The Assyrian army inflicted maximum suffering on its enemies in order to intimidate people who might otherwise resist. (Only individuals who had certain skills or abilities might be spared.)

Assyrian kings took great pride in recording their military conquests in writing (on tablets, clay cylinders, and obelisks) and in pictorial reliefs on stone slabs lining palace walls. Along with a recounting of victories won and plunder taken, archaeologists have found chilling lists of how the Assyrians tortured their captives. These included:

- Flaying (cutting skin into strips and pulling it off a living victim)
- Beheading
- Impaling (inserting a sharpened stake beneath the rib cage of a living victim, putting the stake into the ground so it stood erect, and leaving the victim hanging until the stake pierced a vital organ causing the victim to die)
- Burning people (especially babies and children) alive
- Severing hands, feet, noses, ears, tongues, and testicles
- Gouging out eyes

### THE TRUTH OF THE MATTER

**The Terrible Assyrians**

Their empire was located in Mesopotamia near the Euphrates River.

The Middle Eastern World

The people had such a bad reputation that Jonah fled when God commanded him to speak to Nineveh, Assyria's capital (Jonah 1:1–3).

Known for their ruthlessness in battle and horrific treatment of captives, Assyrian soldiers were equipped with the latest weaponry—barbed arrows, catapults, and siege machines.

The Assyrian army inflicted maximum suffering on its enemies in order to intimidate people who might otherwise resist. (Only individuals who had certain skills or abilities might be spared.)

Assyrian kings took great pride in recording their military conquests in writing (on tablets, clay cylinders, and obelisks) and in pictorial reliefs on stone slabs lining palace walls. Along with a recounting of victories won and plunder taken, archaeologists have found chilling lists of how the Assyrians tortured their captives. These included:

- Flaying (cutting skin into strips and pulling it off a living victim)
- Beheading
- Impaling (inserting a sharpened stake beneath the rib cage of a living victim, putting the stake into the ground so it stood erect, and leaving the victim hanging until the stake pierced a vital organ causing the victim to die)
- Burning people (especially babies and children) alive
- Severing hands, feet, noses, ears, tongues, and testicles
- Gouging out eyes

## ASSYRIA'S CONQUESTS

**The Divided Kingdom**

Circa 740 B.C.  King Tiglath-Pileser began plundering Israel (2 Kings 15:29). He destroyed many cities, brutally killed their inhabitants, and left Israel with only the capital of Samaria intact.

Circa 735 B.C.  King Shalmaneser marched on Samaria after Hoshea—the last king of Israel—refused to pay tribute to the Assyrians. The Assyrians marched on Samaria, slaughtered its inhabitants, and destroyed the remainder of the northern kingdom.

722 B.C.  The ten northern tribes ceased to exist as a people. The Israelites who remained in Israel were forcibly mixed with other religious and ethnic groups and became the hated Samaritans of the New Testament. Those who were deported disappeared from history.

Circa 700 B.C.  The new Assyrian king, Sennacherib, focused his attention on Judah, where he destroyed many cities. (He claimed to have destroyed forty-six walled cities and deported more than 200,000 captives.)

## Small Group Bible Discovery (15 minutes)

*Participant's Guide pages 74–85.*

During this time, a group with fewer than seven participants will stay together. A group with seven or more participants will break into small groups and reassemble as a large group during the final five minutes. Assign each group one of the following topics. If you have more than four small groups, assign some topics to more than one group.

Let's break into groups of three to five—people sitting near you—and study some of the Bible passages and truths mentioned in the video.

Turn to pages 74–85 in your Participant's Guide. There you'll find a list of four topics. You'll have ten minutes to read and discuss the topic I'll assign to you. Choose one person in your group to be a spokesperson for your group when we discuss these topics later.

Assign each group a topic.

I'll signal you when one minute is left.

### ASSYRIA'S CONQUESTS

*Circa 740 B.C.*  King Tiglath-Pileser began plundering Israel (2 Kings 15:29). He destroyed many cities, brutally killed their inhabitants, and left Israel with only the capital of Samaria intact.

*Circa 735 B.C.*  King Shalmaneser marched on Samaria after Hoshea—the last king of Israel—refused to pay tribute to the Assyrians. The Assyrians marched on Samaria, slaughtered its inhabitants, and destroyed the remainder of the northern kingdom.

*722 B.C.*  The ten northern tribes ceased to exist as a people. The Israelites who remained in Israel were forcibly mixed with other religious and ethnic groups and became the hated Samaritans of the New Testament. Those who were deported disappeared from history.

*Circa 700 B.C.*  The new Assyrian king, Sennacherib, focused his attention on Judah, where he destroyed many cities. (He claimed to have destroyed forty-six walled cities and deported more than 200,000 captives.)

**The Divided Kingdom**

## small group Bible Discovery

### Topic A: Guarding the Approaches to Jerusalem

The Israelites lived primarily in the mountains, clustered in towns surrounding Mount Moriah and the city of Jerusalem. After David established his kingdom, Jerusalem became the focal point of the Israelites' religion and their national identity. So, the city needed protection from the enemies of Israel.

1. According to the map of Israel on page 75, which key cities protected access routes to Jerusalem and thus had to be controlled?

2. Even before Jerusalem became the capital of Israel, the Israelites realized they needed to protect the territory surrounding it. Read 1 Samuel 13:23–14:1, 8–15 and note which approach to Jerusalem was threatened and who defended it. Refer to the map on page 75 to help you.

3. According to 1 Samuel 17:1–3, 48–52, where did the Philistines pitch camp? What happened to them after David killed Goliath?

### Topic A: Guarding the Approaches to Jerusalem

The Israelites lived primarily in the mountains, clustered in towns surrounding Mount Moriah and the city of Jerusalem. After David established his kingdom, Jerusalem became the focal point of the Israelites' religion and their national identity. So the city needed protection from the enemies of Israel.

1. According to the map of Israel on page 75, which key cities protected access routes to Jerusalem and thus had to be controlled?

   *Suggested Response:* Micmash, Gezer, Beth Shemesh, Azekah, and Lachish.

2. Even before Jerusalem became the capital of Israel, the Israelites realized they needed to protect the territory surrounding it. Read 1 Samuel 13:23–14:1, 8–15 and note which approach to Jerusalem was threatened and who defended it. Refer to the map on page 75 to help you.

   *Suggested Responses:* The pass by which travelers ascended to Beth Horon was vital to protect. It was guarded by Micmash to the east and Gezer to the west. Jonathan and his armor-bearer attacked the Philistines who had set up an outpost by that pass.

**Topography of Israel**

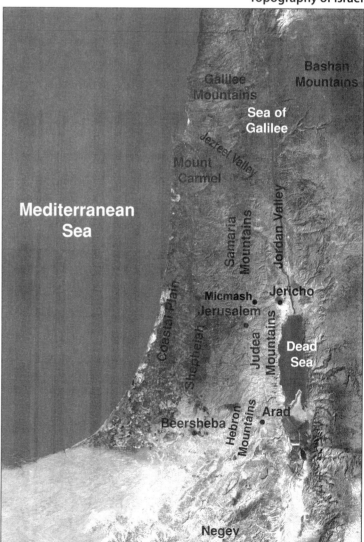

## small Group Bible Discovery

### Topic A: Guarding the Approaches to Jerusalem

The Israelites lived primarily in the mountains, clustered in towns surrounding Mount Moriah and the city of Jerusalem. After David established his kingdom, Jerusalem became the focal point of the Israelites' religion and their national identity. So, the city needed protection from the enemies of Israel.

1. According to the map of Israel on page 75, which key cities protected access routes to Jerusalem and thus had to be controlled?

2. Even before Jerusalem became the capital of Israel, the Israelites realized they needed to protect the territory surrounding it. Read 1 Samuel 13:23–14:1, 8–15 and note which approach to Jerusalem was threatened and who defended it. Refer to the map on page 75 to help you.

3. According to 1 Samuel 17:1–3, 48–52, where did the Philistines pitch camp? What happened to them after David killed Goliath?

4. From which direction did King Sennacherib of Assyria move his army toward Jerusalem? (See Isaiah 36:1–2.)

**Topography of Israel**

3. According to 1 Samuel 17:1–3, 48–52, where did the Philistines pitch camp? What happened to them after David killed Goliath?

   *Suggested Response:* The Philistine army came into the strategic Elah Valley, which was guarded by the city of Azekah. After David killed Goliath, the Philistines fled to the cities of Gath and Ekron.

4. From which direction did King Sennacherib of Assyria move his army toward Jerusalem? (See Isaiah 36:1–2.)

   *Suggested Response:* After conquering Lachish, which guarded the southern flank of Israel, King Sennacherib sent a large army north toward Jerusalem. (Note: Wadi Lachish entered the Hebron Mountains and gave the Assyrians a direct route to Jerusalem.)

5. In the video, Ray Vander Laan pointed out, "It's safe to say that if Lachish stood, Jerusalem would stand; if it fell, Jerusalem would fall." Lachish was a strategic city because it was crucial to the defense of Jerusalem. The relationship between Lachish and Jerusalem illustrates a spiritual truth: we need to defend the less-central issues in order to protect the crucial beliefs and values of the Christian faith. In the chart below, identify some of the "Lachishs" and the "Jerusalems" of our culture.

| The "Lachishs" The less-central issues that must be defended in order to protect the more crucial values | The "Jerusalems" The key beliefs and values of the Christian faith |
| --- | --- |
| | |
| | |
| | |
| | |
| | |
| | |
| | |
| | |

*Note: "Lachishs" mentioned might include standing up for and defending purity and holiness in the face of pornography, integrity in the workplace as opposed to shady dealing, the importance of the marriage vow as opposed to infidelity, standing up for the creation story in the face of evolution theorists, etc. The "Jerusalems" mentioned might include: the sacredness of the family and the marriage union, the high standard of integrity to which God calls Christians, the fact that God created the heavens and the earth, etc.*

4. From which direction did King Sennacherib of Assyria move his army toward Jerusalem? (See Isaiah 36:1–2.)

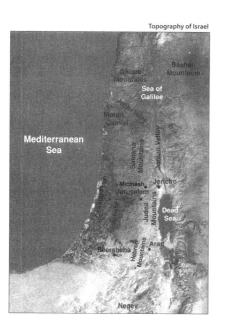

Topography of Israel

5. In the video, Ray Vander Laan pointed out, "It's safe to say that if Lachish stood, Jerusalem would stand; if it fell, Jerusalem would fall." Lachish was a strategic city because it was crucial to the defense of Jerusalem. The relationship between Lachish and Jerusalem illustrates a spiritual truth: we need to defend the less-central issues in order to protect the crucial beliefs and values of the Christian faith. In the chart below, identify some of the "Lachishs" and the "Jerusalems" of our culture.

| The "Lachishs" The less-central issues that must be defended in order to protect the more crucial values | The "Jerusalems" The key beliefs and values of the Christian faith |
| --- | --- |
|  |  |
|  |  |
|  |  |
|  |  |
|  |  |
|  |  |
|  |  |
|  |  |
|  |  |

## EVIDENCE FILE

### Tel Lachish: Its History Unfolds

Israel is dotted with a certain kind of hill called a *tel*. These hills have steep sides, flat tops, and look a bit like coffee tables. They are, in effect, comprised of layers and layers of settlements piled on top of each other. In Jeremiah 30:18, for example, we read about how Jerusalem will be "rebuilt on her ruins." Jeremiah 49:2 describes how Rabbah, an Ammonite city, will become "a mound of ruins."

In general terms, here's how Tel Lachish was formed:

#### Stage 1

People settled on the site, eventually building a wall and gate. Often a rampart was built against the wall to protect the hill from erosion and keep enemies away from the base of the wall.

#### Stage 2

The settlement was abandoned, due to war, drought, etc. Then the ruins faded into the landscape.

#### Stage 3

People moved back to the same spot, filled in holes, gathered larger building stones, leveled off the hill, and rebuilt. Then the city's success attracted enemies . . . and the cycle of destruction continued.

#### Stage 4

Layers upon layers accumulated (sort of like a layer cake), so the hill became higher. Each layer—or stratum—records what life was like during a particular time. Artifacts discovered in the *tel* reveal a great deal about how people lived during particular times.

Tel Lachish—the main setting of this video—reveals the city's rich history. First settled more than 4,000 years before Jesus' birth, it was destroyed and rebuilt at least six times. Between these total destructions, various changes in civilization occurred. For example, the layer of Hezekiah's time (700 B.C.) reveals massive fortification towers, a huge gate complex, and a palace. Another layer contains the remains of the city's fiery destruction (587 B.C.).

Tel Lachish—and other tels—help us to better understand the Bible's message. Each tel is, in effect, a unique gift from God to help us better understand His Word. The insights we gain help us to better understand and interpret the Bible's message.

**Tel Lachish**

## EVIDENCE FILE

### Tel Lachish: Its History Unfolds

Israel is dotted with a certain kind of hill called a *tel*. These hills have steep sides, flat tops, and look a bit like coffee tables. They are, in effect, comprised of layers and layers of settlements piled on top of each other. In Jeremiah 30:18, for example, we read about how Jerusalem will be "rebuilt on her ruins." Jeremiah 49:2 describes how Rabbah, an Ammonite city, will become "a mound of ruins."

In general terms, here's how Tel Lachish was formed:

*Stage 1*

People settled on the site, eventually building a wall and gate. Often a rampart was built against the wall to protect the hill from erosion and keep enemies away from the base of the wall.

*Stage 2*

The settlement was abandoned, due to war, drought, etc. Then the ruins faded into the landscape.

*Stage 3*

People moved back to the same spot, filled in holes, gathered larger building stones, leveled off the hill, and rebuilt. Then the city's success attracted enemies . . . and the cycle of destruction continued.

(continued on page 78)

**Tel Lachish**

(continued from page 77)

*Stage 4*

Layers upon layers accumulated (sort of like a layer cake), so the hill became higher. Each layer—or stratum—records what life was like during a particular time. Artifacts discovered in the *tel* reveal a great deal about how people lived during particular times.

Tel Lachish—the main setting of this video—reveals the city's rich history. First settled more than 4,000 years before Jesus' birth, it was destroyed and rebuilt at least six times. Between these total destructions, various changes in civilization occurred. For example, the layer of Hezekiah's time (700 B.C.) reveals massive fortification towers, a huge gate complex, and a palace. Another layer contains the remains of the city's fiery destruction (587 B.C.).

Tel Lachish—and other tels—help us to better understand the Bible's message. Each tel is, in effect, a unique gift from God to help us better understand His Word. The insights we gain help us to better understand and interpret the Bible's message.

## CONFIRMING EVIDENCE

### The Palace of a Great King

Assyria's kings were committed to more than military conquest. As part of their religious duty, they also constructed massive public buildings. Sennacherib, for example, built a new palace that he named the Palace Without a Rival. His records indicate that the labor force that built it was composed of deportees from many conquered nations (probably including Israel).

This palace, which was discovered during the late nineteenth century, contained more than seventy halls and chambers, all of them lined with stone panels (called *reliefs*) that depicted Sennacherib's accomplishments. Enormous statues of winged bulls guarded the doors of the hallway that led to the main chamber. Hallway walls were lined with panels commemorating the destruction of the cities of Judah, including the siege of Lachish.

> **CONFIRMING EVIDENCE**
>
> **The Palace of a Great King**
>
> Assyria's kings were committed to more than military conquest. As part of their religious duty, they also constructed massive public buildings. Sennacherib, for example, built a new palace that he named the Palace Without a Rival. His records indicate that the labor force that built it was composed of deportees from many conquered nations (probably including Israel).
>
> This palace, which was discovered during the late nineteenth century, contained more than seventy halls and chambers, all of them lined with stone panels (called *reliefs*) that depicted Sennacherib's accomplishments. Enormous statues of winged bulls guarded the doors of the hallway that led to the main chamber. Hallway walls were lined with panels commemorating the destruction of the cities of Judah, including the siege of Lachish.

## Topic B: The Judgment of God

God is incredibly patient with His people, always ready to forgive. But when they are repeatedly rebellious and refuse to heed His warnings, He will send judgment.

1.  What cautions did God give the Israelites soon after they entered Canaan? (See Deuteronomy 8:11–20.)

    *Suggested Responses:* Do not forget Him, keep His laws and decrees, remember what He had done for them, do not become proud in their affluence because their wealth had come from Him. Also, if they served other gods, they would perish.

2.  What did God promise would happen if the Israelites failed to obey Him? (See Deuteronomy 28:15, 21–22, 49–52, 62–63.)

    *Suggested Responses:* They would be cursed and struck with diseases, drought, scorching heat, and other problems. Their enemies would defeat them, and God would allow a fierce nation to ruin all the cities and land that He had given them and cause many of them to perish.

3.  Which sins did the Israelites commit that finally brought God's judgment? (See 2 Kings 17:9–17.)

    *Suggested Responses:* They worshiped other gods and followed the practices of pagan people such as building high places, setting up sacred stones and Asherah poles, burning incense at the high places, practicing witchcraft and sorcery, making idols, sacrificing their children, and worshiping the heavens. Despite the repeated warnings of God's prophets, the Israelites completely rejected all of God's commandments and "sold themselves to do evil in the eyes of the LORD."

*(continued from page 77)*

### Stage 4

Layers upon layers accumulated (sort of like a layer cake), so the hill became higher. Each layer—or stratum—records what life was like during a particular time. Artifacts discovered in the *tel* reveal a great deal about how people lived during particular times.

Tel Lachish—the main setting of this video—reveals the city's rich history. First settled more than 4,000 years before Jesus' birth, it was destroyed and rebuilt at least six times. Between these total destructions, various changes in civilization occurred. For example, the layer of Hezekiah's time (700 B.C.) reveals massive fortification towers, a huge gate complex, and a palace. Another layer contains the remains of the city's fiery destruction (587 B.C.).

Tel Lachish—and other tels—help us to better understand the Bible's message. Each tel is, in effect, a unique gift from God to help us better understand His Word. The insights we gain help us to better understand and interpret the Bible's message.

### CONFIRMING EVIDENCE

#### The Palace of a Great King

Assyria's kings were committed to more than military conquest. As part of their religious duty, they also constructed massive public buildings. Sennacherib, for example, built a new palace that he named the Palace Without a Rival. His records indicate that the labor force that built it was composed of deportees from many conquered nations (probably including Israel).

This palace, which was discovered during the late nineteenth century, contained more than seventy halls and chambers, all of them lined with stone panels (called *reliefs*) that depicted Sennacherib's accomplishments. Enormous statues of winged bulls guarded the doors of the hallway that led to the main chamber. Hallway walls were lined with panels commemorating the destruction of the cities of Judah, including the siege of Lachish.

### Topic B: The Judgment of God

God is incredibly patient with His people, always ready to forgive. But when they are repeatedly rebellious and refuse to heed His warnings, He will send judgment.

1. What cautions did God give the Israelites soon after they entered Canaan? (See Deuteronomy 8:11–20.)

2. What did God promise would happen if the Israelites failed to obey Him? (See Deuteronomy 28:15, 21–22, 49–52, 62–63.)

3. Which sins did the Israelites commit that finally brought God's judgment? (See 2 Kings 17:9–17.)

4. After Israel was divided, God sent His prophets to both Israel and Judah. Look up the following verses and take note of the message each prophet delivered.

| Jeremiah 1:14–16 | The Prophet | |
| | The Kingdom | |
| | The Message | |
| Hosea 10:1–2, 5–10 | The Prophet | |
| | The Kingdom | |
| | The Message | |

✏ 4.  After Israel was divided, God sent His prophets to both Israel and Judah. Look up the following verses and take note of the message each prophet delivered.

| Jeremiah 1:14–16 | The Prophet | *Jeremiah* |
|---|---|---|
| | The Kingdom | *Judah* |
| | The Message | *Foreign kings would "pour out" disaster on them because of the Israelites' wickedness in forsaking God.* |
| Hosea 10:1–2, 5–10 | The Prophet | *Hosea* |
| | The Kingdom | *Israel* |
| | The Message | *They would have to bear the guilt for their deceitful hearts. Their calf-idol would be taken to Assyria as tribute, Israel would be ashamed of its idols, Samaria and its king would be removed, and nations would put the Israelites into bondage.* |

✏ 5.  What did God allow the Assyrians to do to Israel because of their failure to keep His commandments? (See 2 Kings 17:18–23.)

*Suggested Response:* He rejected Israel and removed the people from His presence by giving them over to Assyria, which plundered the land and carried the people away to Assyria.

**Topic B: The Judgment of God**

God is incredibly patient with His people, always ready to forgive. But when they are repeatedly rebellious and refuse to heed His warnings, He will send judgment.

1. What cautions did God give the Israelites soon after they entered Canaan? (See Deuteronomy 8:11–20.)

2. What did God promise would happen if the Israelites failed to obey Him? (See Deuteronomy 28:15, 21–22, 49–52, 62–63.)

3. Which sins did the Israelites commit that finally brought God's judgment? (See 2 Kings 17:9–17.)

4. After Israel was divided, God sent His prophets to both Israel and Judah. Look up the following verses and take note of the message each prophet delivered.

| Jeremiah 1:14–16 | The Prophet | |
| | The Kingdom | |
| | The Message | |
| Hosea 10:1–2, 5–10 | The Prophet | |
| | The Kingdom | |
| | The Message | |

5. What did God allow the Assyrians to do to Israel because of their failure to keep His commandments? (See 2 Kings 17:18–23.)

---

**WORTH OBSERVING**

**God Punishes People for Their Sins**

The biblical reality that God hates sin and will eventually punish it is reinforced in the stories of the Flood, Sodom and Gomorrah, the conquest of Canaan, and the exile of the Israelites.

*God's Judgment*

God made the Sabbath principle central to His creation. As part of their recognition that God owned everything, the Israelites were to set apart the seventh day for the Lord. To violate the Sabbath day was a serious sin because it denied God's sovereignty. Also, every seventh year the land was to lie fallow and not be farmed (Leviticus 25:1–7). Yahweh promised to provide an abundant crop in the sixth year so no one would be hungry during the following year.

But the Israelites' illicit affair with pagan gods started almost as soon as they arrived in Canaan. Because idolatry did not acknowledge Him as the one true God, God condemned it. He knew that idol worshipers would work on the Sabbath day because they would not recognize that they belonged to God and that God owned the land. So He told them, in Leviticus 26:35, that if they continued to be disobedient He would take their land from them so it would "have the rest it did not have during the sabbaths you lived in it."

The Israelites' continued disobedience finally caused God to bring judgment on them. (See 2 Kings 17:18–20 and 2 Chronicles 36:15–20.) He ripped His stiff-necked people from their land, asserting His ownership over it and them (2 Chronicles 36:21). In 722 B.C., the Assyrians destroyed the people of Israel (the northern ten tribes). In 586 B.C., the

## WORTH OBSERVING

### God Punishes People for Their Sins

The biblical reality that God hates sin and will eventually punish it is reinforced in the stories of the Flood, Sodom and Gomorrah, the conquest of Canaan, and the exile of the Israelites.

#### God's Judgment

God made the Sabbath principle central to His creation. As part of their recognition that God owned everything, the Israelites were to set apart the seventh day for the Lord. To violate the Sabbath day was a serious sin because it denied God's sovereignty. Also, every seventh year the land was to lie fallow and not be farmed (Leviticus 25:1–7). Yahweh promised to provide an abundant crop in the sixth year so no one would be hungry during the following year.

But the Israelites' illicit affair with pagan gods started almost as soon as they arrived in Canaan. Because idolatry did not acknowledge Him as the one true God, God condemned it. He knew that idol worshipers would work on the Sabbath day because they would not recognize that they belonged to God and that God owned the land. So He told them, in Leviticus 26:35, that if they continued to be disobedient He would take their land from them so it would "have the rest it did not have during the sabbaths you lived in it."

The Israelites' continued disobedience finally caused God to bring judgment on them. (See 2 Kings 17:18–20 and 2 Chronicles 36:15–20.) He ripped His stiff-necked people from their land, asserting His ownership over it and them (2 Chronicles 36:21). In 722 B.C., the Assyrians destroyed the people of Israel (the northern ten tribes). In 586 B.C., the people of Judah were exiled to Babylon for seventy years—and the land rested for seventy years.

#### The Hope Promised

Although God allowed Assyria to take the people of Judah into exile, He did not forsake His people, nor did He end His plan for their redemption. Second Chronicles 36:22–23 ends with optimism because the Israelites would return to their land and the temple would be rebuilt.

As it turned out, God's people experienced tremendous spiritual growth during the Babylonian Captivity (586 B.C.). Without their temple, the Israelites learned that obedience is better than sacrifice (Psalm 40:6 and Isaiah 1:10–20). They learned the importance of obeying all of God's commands or suffering the consequences. The Israelites returned from Babylon with a renewed focus on God and the need to be faithful to Him (Ezra 9:10–15). Never again would Baal worship and the shedding of innocent blood be the religion of the nation.

5.  What did God allow the Assyrians to do to Israel because of their failure to keep His commandments? (See 2 Kings 17:18–23.)

## WORTH OBSERVING

### God Punishes People for Their Sins

The biblical reality that God hates sin and will eventually punish it is reinforced in the stories of the Flood, Sodom and Gomorrah, the conquest of Canaan, and the exile of the Israelites.

#### God's Judgment

God made the Sabbath principle central to His creation. As part of their recognition that God owned everything, the Israelites were to set apart the seventh day for the Lord. To violate the Sabbath day was a serious sin because it denied God's sovereignty. Also, every seventh year the land was to lie fallow and not be farmed (Leviticus 25:1–7). Yahweh promised to provide an abundant crop in the sixth year so no one would be hungry during the following year.

But the Israelites' illicit affair with pagan gods started almost as soon as they arrived in Canaan. Because idolatry did not acknowledge Him as the one true God, God condemned it. He knew that idol worshipers would work on the Sabbath day because they would not recognize that they belonged to God and that God owned the land. So He told them, in Leviticus 26:35, that if they continued to be disobedient He would take their land from them so it would "have the rest it did not have during the sabbaths you lived in it."

The Israelites' continued disobedience finally caused God to bring judgment on them. (See 2 Kings 17:18–20 and 2 Chronicles 36:15–20.) He ripped His stiff-necked people from their land, asserting His ownership over it and them (2 Chronicles 36:21). In 722 B.C., the Assyrians destroyed the people of Israel (the northern ten tribes). In 586 B.C., the

people of Judah were exiled to Babylon for seventy years—and the land rested for seventy years.

#### The Hope Promised

Although God allowed Assyria to take the people of Judah into exile, He did not forsake His people, nor did He end His plan for their redemption. Second Chronicles 36:22–23 ends with optimism because the Israelites would return to their land and the temple would be rebuilt.

As it turned out, God's people experienced tremendous spiritual growth during the Babylonian Captivity (586 B.C.). Without their temple, the Israelites learned that obedience is better than sacrifice (Psalm 40:6 and Isaiah 1:10–20). They learned the importance of obeying all of God's commands or suffering the consequences. The Israelites returned from Babylon with a renewed focus on God and the need to be faithful to Him (Ezra 9:10–15). Never again would Baal worship and the shedding of innocent blood be the religion of the nation.

### Topic C: Four Kings Who Prolonged God's Patience

In 722 B.C., the ten northern tribes of Israel were destroyed when God punished them for forsaking Him. The southern kingdom of Judah, however, continued to exist for more than a century before receiving God's judgment at the hands of the Babylonians. Why did Judah last so much longer than Israel? Consider the work of several, God-fearing kings who brought the people of Judah back—at least temporarily—from the brink of disaster.

#### King Asa

1.  What did King Asa do that pleased God? What was the result? (See 2 Chronicles 14:2–7.)

## Topic C: Four Kings Who Prolonged God's Patience

In 722 B.C., the ten northern tribes of Israel were destroyed when God punished them for forsaking Him. The southern kingdom of Judah, however, continued to exist for more than a century before receiving God's judgment at the hands of the Babylonians. Why did Judah last so much longer than Israel? Consider the work of several, God-fearing kings who brought the people of Judah back—at least temporarily—from the brink of disaster.

### King Asa

1.  What did King Asa do that pleased God? What was the result? (See 2 Chronicles 14:2–7.)

    *Suggested Responses:* King Asa removed foreign altars and high places, smashed sacred stones, cut down Asherah poles, and commanded his people to seek God and to obey His laws and commands. The people prospered and fortified Judah's cities because God gave them rest from their enemies.

2.  What did God promise King Asa, through the prophet Azariah? (See 2 Chronicles 15:1–2.)

    *Suggested Responses:* God promised to be with Asa as long as the king sought Him. But if the king forsook God, God would forsake him.

3.  In what ways did King Asa encourage his people to seek the Lord? (See 2 Chronicles 15:8–16.)

    *Suggested Responses:* He removed the idols from the land and repaired the altar of the Lord. Then he assembled all the people at Jerusalem, where they sacrificed to God and entered into a covenant to seek Him wholeheartedly. Anyone who would not seek the Lord was to be killed. Asa also deposed the queen mother because she had made an Asherah pole.

4.  What was King Asa's great act of foolishness later in his life? How did God respond? (See 2 Chronicles 16:1–9.)

    *Suggested Responses:* Instead of relying on God when King Baasha of Israel began to fortify against him, King Asa took silver and gold from the Lord's temple in order to pay for the help of Ben-Hadad king of Aram. As a result, God allowed the army of Ben-Hadad to escape judgment and promised King Asa that Judah would be at war perpetually.

### King Joash

5.  What did King Joash do to turn the people back toward God? (See 2 Chronicles 24:8–9, 12–14.)

    *Suggested Response:* He commanded the people to pay taxes to repair the ruined temple in Jerusalem. During his reign, the temple repairs were completed and burnt offerings were once again made in the temple.

6.  What did King Joash do after the death of Jehoiada, the chief priest? What was the result? (See 2 Chronicles 24:17–21, 23–25.)

    *Suggested Responses:* At the bidding of his leaders, he worshiped idols and Asherah poles and killed a prophet, Zechariah, whom God had sent to him. God

people of Judah were exiled to Babylon for seventy years—and the land rested for seventy years.

***The Hope Promised***

Although God allowed Assyria to take the people of Judah into exile, He did not forsake His people, nor did He end His plan for their redemption. Second Chronicles 36:22–23 ends with optimism because the Israelites would return to their land and the temple would be rebuilt.

As it turned out, God's people experienced tremendous spiritual growth during the Babylonian Captivity (586 B.C.). Without their temple, the Israelites learned that obedience is better than sacrifice (Psalm 40:6 and Isaiah 1:10–20). They learned the importance of obeying all of God's commands or suffering the consequences. The Israelites returned from Babylon with a renewed focus on God and the need to be faithful to Him (Ezra 9:10–15). Never again would Baal worship and the shedding of innocent blood be the religion of the nation.

### Topic C: Four Kings Who Prolonged God's Patience

In 722 B.C., the ten northern tribes of Israel were destroyed when God punished them for forsaking Him. The southern kingdom of Judah, however, continued to exist for more than a century before receiving God's judgment at the hands of the Babylonians. Why did Judah last so much longer than Israel? Consider the work of several, God-fearing kings who brought the people of Judah back—at least temporarily—from the brink of disaster.

*King Asa*

1. What did King Asa do that pleased God? What was the result? (See 2 Chronicles 14:2–7.)

2. What did God promise King Asa, through the prophet Azariah? (See 2 Chronicles 15:1–2.)

3. In what ways did King Asa encourage his people to seek the Lord? (See 2 Chronicles 15:8–16.)

4. What was King Asa's great act of foolishness later in his life? How did God respond? (See 2 Chronicles 16:1–9.)

*King Joash*

5. What did King Joash do to turn the people back toward God? (See 2 Chronicles 24:8–9, 12–14.)

6. What did King Joash do after the death of Jehoiada, the chief priest? What was the result? (See 2 Chronicles 24:17–21, 23–25.)

allowed the army of Aram to invade Judah and Jerusalem and kill all the people's leaders. When the Arameans withdrew from battle, Joash's officials killed him in his bed because he had murdered God's prophet.

### King Hezekiah

7.  How would you describe Hezekiah's spiritual insight and commitment to God? (See 2 Chronicles 29:1–10.)

    *Suggested Responses:* Hezekiah had keen spiritual insight. He realized that his ancestors had been unfaithful to God and had forsaken Him. Consequently, God's anger had fallen on Judah and Jerusalem and brought many negative consequences. He desired to do right in the sight of God and to make a covenant with God so that God's anger would turn away from them.

8.  What did Hezekiah do to restore the people's relationship with Yahweh? What were the results? (See 2 Chronicles 29:3–5, 20–24, 35–36; 31:1.)

    *Suggested Responses:* Hezekiah commanded that the temple be repaired and purified. After that was done, he gathered city officials together, who brought animals for a sin offering. He then commanded the priests to sacrifice the animals to atone for all Israel. As a result, the temple was once again used for worship, and people reestablished a vibrant relationship with Yahweh. They smashed sacred stones, cut down Asherah poles, and destroyed pagan high places and altars throughout Judah, Benjamin, Ephraim, and Manasseh.

### King Josiah

9.  Instead of following false gods, what did King Josiah do? What was the result? (See 2 Chronicles 34:3–8, 14, 21–33.)

    *Suggested Responses:* Josiah supervised the destruction of Baal altars, incense altars, Asherah poles, and the bones of the false priests. He assigned people to repair the temple, where the Book of the Law was discovered. When the book was read to him, he was distraught because he knew God's wrath would be poured out on the people because of their disobedience. So the king read all the words of the book to the people assembled at the temple, pledged himself to follow and obey God, and then had everyone else in Jerusalem and Benjamin pledge themselves, too. Because of his heart for God, God promised that Josiah would be spared from the coming evil.

## Topic D: Hezekiah—Prepared to Defend God's People

1.  According to 2 Chronicles 31:20–21, how did God respond to Hezekiah's faithfulness?

    *Suggested Response: God allowed Hezekiah and his people to prosper.*

2.  Although Hezekiah had undertaken one of the greatest religious reforms the nation of Israel had ever seen, God still judged the culture for its sinfulness. What did God allow to happen? (See 2 Chronicles 32:1, 9.)

    *Suggested Response:* Sennacherib, king of Assyria, invaded Judah and laid siege to the fortified cities there, including Lachish.

*King Hezekiah*

7. How would you describe Hezekiah's spiritual insight and commitment to God? (See 2 Chronicles 29:1–10.)

8. What did Hezekiah do to restore the people's relationship with Yahweh? What were the results? (See 2 Chronicles 29:3–5, 20–24, 35–36; 31:1.)

*King Josiah*

9. Instead of following false gods, what did King Josiah do? What was the result? (See 2 Chronicles 34:3–8, 14, 21–33.)

---

**Topic D: Hezekiah—Prepared to Defend God's People**

1. According to 2 Chronicles 31:20–21, how did God respond to Hezekiah's faithfulness?

2. Although Hezekiah had undertaken one of the greatest religious reforms the nation of Israel had ever seen, God still judged the culture for its sinfulness. What did God allow to happen? (See 2 Chronicles 32:1, 9.)

3. After Sennacherib, Assyria's king, invaded Judah with plans to attack the fortified cities of Judah, what plans did Hezekiah implement? How did he encourage his people? (See 2 Chronicles 32:2–8.)

4. How did Sennacherib respond to Hezekiah and the Israelites' God? (See 2 Chronicles 32:9–19 and Isaiah 36:12–18.)

---

**PLANNING NOTES:**

3.  After Sennacherib, Assyria's king, invaded Judah with plans to attack the fortified cities of Judah, what plans did Hezekiah implement? How did he encourage his people? (See 2 Chronicles 32:2–8.)

*Suggested Responses:* Hezekiah blocked up all the springs of water outside the city of Jerusalem, built a tunnel to carry water from the springs into Jerusalem, repaired broken sections of the city wall, and built towers on the wall. He also made many weapons and shields, and appointed military officers to rule the people. To encourage the people, Hezekiah told them not to be afraid or discouraged because God, who was greater than the king of Assyria, was with them and would fight their battles.

4.  How did Sennacherib respond to Hezekiah and the Israelites' God? (See 2 Chronicles 32:9–19 and Isaiah 36:12–18.)

*Suggested Responses:* Sennacherib challenged Hezekiah and his God, mocked what Hezekiah had done to remove high places and altars, and ridiculed the power of God and the people's faith in God. After telling the people that they'd have to eat their own human waste, Sennacherib's commander urged the people to make peace with the Assyrians and said that Sennacherib would take them to a "land of grain and new wine, a land of bread and vineyards."

5.  What was Hezekiah's response to Sennacherib's challenges and mockery? (See Isaiah 37:1, 14–20.)

*Suggested Responses:* Hezekiah put on sackcloth and entered the temple. There he turned the matter over to God. The king acknowledged God's greatness and stated that he wanted God to deliver the people from Assyria so that "all kingdoms on earth may know" that God alone was God.

**The First Temple at Jerusalem**

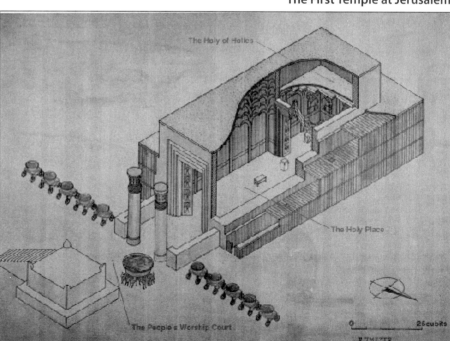

**Topic D: Hezekiah—Prepared to Defend God's People**

1. According to 2 Chronicles 31:20–21, how did God respond to Hezekiah's faithfulness?

2. Although Hezekiah had undertaken one of the greatest religious reforms the nation of Israel had ever seen, God still judged the culture for its sinfulness. What did God allow to happen? (See 2 Chronicles 32:1, 9.)

3. After Sennacherib, Assyria's king, invaded Judah with plans to attack the fortified cities of Judah, what plans did Hezekiah implement? How did he encourage his people? (See 2 Chronicles 32:2–8.)

4. How did Sennacherib respond to Hezekiah and the Israelites' God? (See 2 Chronicles 32:9–19 and Isaiah 36:12–18.)

5. What was Hezekiah's response to Sennacherib's challenges and mockery? (See Isaiah 37:1, 14–20.)

**The First Temple at Jerusalem**

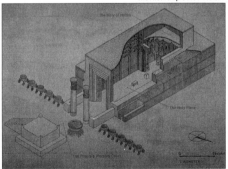

6. How did God respond to Hezekiah's prayer? (Isaiah 37:21–22a, 33–37)

✏ 6.    How did God respond to Hezekiah's prayer? (Isaiah 37:21–22a, 33–37.)

*Suggested Responses:* God heard Hezekiah's prayer and honored his faith. God promised that Jerusalem would be spared, then the angel of the Lord killed 185,000 Assyrian soldiers in their camp outside Jerusalem.

## DATA FILE

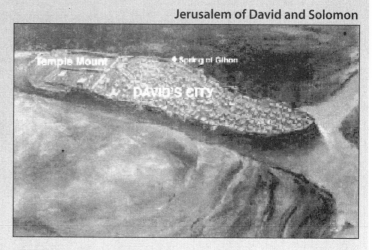

Jerusalem of David and Solomon

### Hezekiah's Amazing Water System

The spring of Gihon, which flowed out of a cave on the eastern side of the hill on which Jerusalem was built, provided the city's main water supply. (More than 24,250 cubic feet of water per day still flow from it.) As long as the cave's entrance was outside the city walls, the city's water supply was vulnerable to disruption by enemies.

Before David captured the city in about 1000 B.C., the Jebusites living there dug a shaft from the city into the cave. Quite possibly Joab, David's commander, captured the city by entering the cave and climbing up the shaft. (See 2 Samuel 5:8 and 1 Chronicles 11:6.)

Although Hezekiah trusted God totally (Isaiah 37:14–20), he resolved to do everything possible to prepare his people to face the Assyrians. When he heard about the Assyrians' arrival, he ordered his workers to dig a tunnel from the cave through the ridge on which the city was built in order to bring water to the western side of the ridge—to the pool of Siloam within the city walls. Then he covered up the cave's opening (2 Kings 20:20; 2 Chronicles 32:2–4). Today, this extraordinary accomplishment—built more than 700 years before Jesus walked on the earth—still ranks as one of the engineering marvels of the ancient world. Here's why:

Hezekiah's Water Tunnel

- Two teams of workmen, working from both directions, chiseled a tunnel barely two feet wide through solid rock, sometimes at points more than 150 feet underground, and met in the middle. And they did this without modern tools or instruments!
- The tunnel is 1,748 feet long and has a drop of just 12 inches.
- Water more than waist deep still flows through the tunnel.
- In 1880, boys playing in the tunnel discovered writing chiseled into the ceiling. Called the Siloam Inscription, it describes the dramatic moment when the two teams of workers met. Today, the inscription is in the Istanbul Archaeological Museum, having been removed from the tunnel when the Turks ruled Palestine during the late nineteenth century.

## DATA FILE

### Hezekiah's Amazing Water System

The spring of Gihon, which flowed out of a cave on the eastern side of the hill on which Jerusalem was built, provided the city's main water supply. (More than 24,250 cubic feet of water per day still flow from it.) As long as the cave's entrance was outside the city walls, the city's water supply was vulnerable to disruption by enemies.

Before David captured the city in about 1000 B.C., the Jebusites living there dug a shaft from the city into the cave. Quite possibly Joab, David's commander, captured the city by entering the cave and climbing up the shaft. (See 2 Samuel 5:8 and 1 Chronicles 11:6.)

**Jerusalem of David and Solomon**

Although Hezekiah trusted God totally (Isaiah 37:14–20), he resolved to do everything possible to prepare his people to face the Assyrians. When he heard about the Assyrians' arrival, he ordered his workers to dig a tunnel from the cave through the ridge on which the city was built in order to bring water to the western side of the ridge—to the pool of Siloam within the city walls. Then he covered up the cave's opening (2 Kings 20:20; 2 Chronicles 32:2–4). Today, this extraordinary accomplishment—built more than 700 years before Jesus walked on the earth—still ranks as one of the engineering marvels of the ancient world. Here's why:

- Two teams of workmen, working from both directions, chiseled a tunnel barely two feet wide through solid rock, sometimes at points

more than 150 feet underground, and met in the middle. And they did this without modern tools or instruments!
- The tunnel is 1,748 feet long and has a drop of just 12 inches.
- Water more than waist deep still flows through the tunnel.
- In 1880, boys playing in the tunnel discovered writing chiseled into the ceiling. Called the Siloam Inscription, it describes the dramatic moment when the two teams of workers met. Today, the inscription is in the Istanbul Archaeological Museum, having been removed from the tunnel when the Turks ruled Palestine during the late nineteenth century.

**Hezekiah's Water Tunnel**

> After nine minutes, let participants know that they have one minute remaining. Then reassemble the entire group. After everyone is back together, begin asking one person from each small group to briefly share a key idea with the larger group. In some cases, you may not have time for every group to share their discoveries.

As time allows, let's briefly share the key ideas that your group discussed.

# ꜰaith ʟesson

**8** minutes

## Time for Reflection (5 minutes)

On page 88 of your Participant's Guide, you'll find a passage of Scripture. Let's each read this passage silently and take the next few minutes to consider how God deals with a culture that refuses to obey Him.

Please do not talk during this time. It's a time when we all can reflect on today's lesson and how it applies to our lives.

> *The Scripture passage and questions are reproduced in their entirety in the Participant's Guide on pages 88–89.*

Zedekiah was twenty-one years old when he became king, and he reigned in Jerusalem eleven years. He did evil in the eyes of the LORD his God and did not humble himself before Jeremiah the prophet, who spoke the word of the LORD. He also rebelled against King Nebuchadnezzar, who had made him take an oath in God's name. He became stiff-necked and hardened his heart and would not turn to the LORD, the God of Israel. Furthermore, all the leaders of the priests and the people became more and more unfaithful, following all the detestable practices of the nations and defiling the temple of the LORD, which he had consecrated in Jerusalem. The LORD, the God of their fathers, sent word to them through his messengers again and again, because he had pity on his people and on his dwelling place. But they mocked God's messengers, despised his words and scoffed at his prophets until the wrath of the LORD was aroused against his people and there was no remedy. He brought up against them the king of the Babylonians, who killed their young men with the sword in the sanctuary, and spared neither young man nor young woman, old man or aged. God handed all of them over to Nebuchadnezzar. . . . until the seventy years were completed in fulfillment of the word of the LORD spoken by Jeremiah.

2 CHRONICLES 36:11–17, 21

1.  In what ways has your knowledge of God—His hatred of sin, His willingness to forgive, His judgment—changed as a result of this study?

2.  Which issues today may not seem terribly important, yet must be defended in order to protect the more crucial values?

## faith Lesson

### Time for Reflection

Read the following passage of Scripture and take the next few minutes to consider how God deals with a culture that refuses to obey Him.

> Zedekiah was twenty-one years old when he became king, and he reigned in Jerusalem eleven years. He did evil in the eyes of the LORD his God and did not humble himself before Jeremiah the prophet, who spoke the word of the LORD. He also rebelled against King Nebuchadnezzar, who had made him take an oath in God's name. He became stiff-necked and hardened his heart and would not turn to the LORD, the God of Israel. Furthermore, all the leaders of the priests and the people became more and more unfaithful, following all the detestable practices of the nations and defiling the temple of the LORD, which he had consecrated in Jerusalem. The LORD, the God of their fathers, sent word to them through his messengers again and again, because he had pity on his people and on his dwelling place. But they mocked God's messengers, despised his words and scoffed at his prophets until the wrath of the LORD was aroused against his people and there was no remedy. He brought up against them the king of the Babylonians, who killed their young men with the sword in the sanctuary, and spared neither young man nor young woman, old man or aged. God handed all of them over to Nebuchadnezzar.... until the seventy years were completed in fulfillment of the word of the LORD spoken by Jeremiah.
>
> 2 CHRONICLES 36:11–17, 21

1. In what ways has your knowledge of God—His hatred of sin, His willingness to forgive, His judgment—changed as a result of this study?

2. Which issues today may not seem terribly important, yet must be defended in order to protect the more crucial values?

3. Just as the people of Israel and Judah descended into unfaithfulness by taking small steps, so Christians today find themselves becoming unfaithful to God in small but significant ways. In what way(s) have you taken small steps away from God? What were (or are) the consequences?

4. To follow God faithfully, you must be willing to destroy any "high places" (sinful practices, habits, and "gods") to which you are devoted. Which "high place" in your life needs to be confronted and destroyed?

### Action Points

Take a moment to review the key points you explored today, then jot down an action step (or steps) that you will commit to this week as a result of what you have learned.

1. *When a culture fails to live out its God-given calling and disobeys the standards found in His Word, God may send judgment on the entire culture—those who are godly as well as those who persist in wrongdoing.*

   For generations, Israel and Judah disobeyed God repeatedly even though He kept calling them back to Himself. They persisted in idol worship and refused to commit

✏ 3.   Just as the people of Israel and Judah descended into unfaithfulness by taking small steps, so Christians today find themselves becoming unfaithful to
God in small but significant ways. In what way(s) have you taken small steps
away from God? What were (or are) the consequences?

✏ 4.   To follow God faithfully, you must be willing to destroy any "high places"
(sinful practices, habits, and "gods") to which you are devoted. Which "high
place" in your life needs to be confronted and destroyed?

## Action Points (3 minutes)

> *The following points are reproduced on pages 89–90 of the Participant's Guide:*

Now it's time to wrap up our session.

> Give participants a moment to transition from their thoughtfulness to giving
> you their full attention.

I'd like to take a moment to summarize the key points we explored. After I
have reviewed these points, I will give you a moment to jot down an action step
(or steps) that you will commit to this week as a result of what you have learned
today.

> Read the following points and pause afterward so that participants can con-
> sider and write out their commitment.

✏ 1.   *When a culture fails to live out its God-given calling and disobeys the standards found in His Word, God may send judgment on the entire culture—
those who are godly as well as those who persist in wrongdoing.*

For generations, Israel and Judah disobeyed God repeatedly even though He
kept calling them back to Himself. They persisted in idol worship and
refused to commit themselves to Him and to the lifestyle He requires. So
God finally sent judgment in the form of the Assyrian army.

**For which particular sins might God choose to judge your entire culture
if it remains unrepentant?**

✏ 2.   *It is God's desire that those who love Him make an impact on their culture.*
Those who are wholly devoted to God and are willing to stand against evil
can be very effective in redeeming the culture.

Because of Hezekiah's faithful devotion to God, he was able to impact his
culture in godly ways and ultimately helped to bring about God's purposes
in the world—Jesus' lineage through the tribe of Judah. At the heart of his
effectiveness was the fact that Hezekiah did what was right, prepared for the
difficulties to come while trusting God completely, and truly desired that
the world would know that God is God.

2. Which issues today may not seem terribly important, yet must be defended in order to protect the more crucial values?

3. Just as the people of Israel and Judah descended into unfaithfulness by taking small steps, so Christians today find themselves becoming unfaithful to God in small but significant ways. In what way(s) have you taken small steps away from God? What were (or are) the consequences?

4. To follow God faithfully, you must be willing to destroy any "high places" (sinful practices, habits, and "gods") to which you are devoted. Which "high place" in your life needs to be confronted and destroyed?

**Action Points**

Take a moment to review the key points you explored today, then jot down an action step (or steps) that you will commit to this week as a result of what you have learned.

1. *When a culture fails to live out its God-given calling and disobeys the standards found in His Word, God may send judgment on the entire culture—those who are godly as well as those who persist in wrongdoing.*

   For generations, Israel and Judah disobeyed God repeatedly even though He kept calling them back to Himself. They persisted in idol worship and refused to commit

themselves to Him and to the lifestyle He requires. So God finally sent judgment in the form of the Assyrian army.

**For which particular sins might God choose to judge your entire culture if it remains unrepentant?**

2. *It is God's desire that those who love Him make an impact on their culture. Those who are wholly devoted to God and are willing to stand against evil can be very effective in redeeming the culture.*

   Because of Hezekiah's faithful devotion to God, he was able to impact his culture in godly ways and ultimately helped to bring about God's purposes in the world—Jesus' lineage through the tribe of Judah. At the heart of his effectiveness was the fact that Hezekiah did what was right, prepared for the difficulties to come while trusting God completely, and truly desired that the world would know that God is God.

   **In what specific way(s) are you—like the people of Lachish—content to absorb the sinful values of secular society instead of standing firm for God, trusting Him, and being His instrument in your world?**

   What specific steps might God be calling you to take in order to impact your culture for Him, so that the world will continue to know that God is God?

PLANNING NOTES:

In what specific way(s) are you—like the people of Lachish—content to absorb the sinful values of secular society instead of standing firm for God, trusting Him, and being His instrument in your world?

What specific steps might God be calling you to take in order to impact your culture for Him, so that the world will continue to know that God is God?

# closing prayer

1 minute

The events at Lachish show that God takes sin seriously, yet He gives His people many opportunities to repent of their sins before sending judgment. Let's leave here today thinking about the sins in our lives that need to be addressed, and also how willing we are to be used by God to confront the evils in our culture.

*Dear God, we know that Your judgment will certainly fall on those who persist in wrongdoing. Please help us to face our sins and get right with You. Help us to faithfully trust You, like Hezekiah did, so we can impact our culture in godly ways and demonstrate to people around us that You alone are God. Amen.*

themselves to Him and to the lifestyle He requires. So God finally sent judgment in the form of the Assyrian army.

**For which particular sins might God choose to judge your entire culture if it remains unrepentant?**

2. *It is God's desire that those who love Him make an impact on their culture. Those who are wholly devoted to God and are willing to stand against evil can be very effective in redeeming the culture.*

Because of Hezekiah's faithful devotion to God, he was able to impact his culture in godly ways and ultimately helped to bring about God's purposes in the world—Jesus' lineage through the tribe of Judah. At the heart of his effectiveness was the fact that Hezekiah did what was right, prepared for the difficulties to come while trusting God completely, and truly desired that the world would know that God is God.

**In what specific way(s) are you—like the people of Lachish—content to absorb the sinful values of secular society instead of standing firm for God, trusting Him, and being His instrument in your world?**

**What specific steps might God be calling you to take in order to impact your culture for Him, so that the world will continue to know that God is God?**

# The Lord is my shepherd

## Before you lead

### Synopsis

Throughout Scripture, God is presented as our Good Shepherd—a concept that is foreign to most Westerners. Filmed in the "Negev," the southern desert area of Israel, this video will help viewers understand and appreciate God's presentation of Himself as our Shepherd. In addition, the video provides insight into the Israelites' wilderness experience, which is the source of much of the Bible's imagery and teaching.

Because of their nomadic wanderings in the desert prior to entering Canaan, the Israelites thought of themselves as wilderness or desert people. Abraham, Isaac, Joseph, Moses, and even King David lived and worked in the desert for periods of time. In fact, the ancestors of the Hebrew people lived in much the same way as the seminomadic Bedouin people shown in this video live today. They lived in tents, raised sheep and goats, and moved from place to place to feed their flocks. Long after the Hebrews had settled in the more hospitable land of Canaan, their wilderness experience continued to shape their identity. Thus the wilderness played a significant role in shaping biblical history and the images and metaphors that God used to describe Himself and His relationship with His people.

In order for us to appreciate the rich images of Scripture, we must remember that the inspired writers of the Bible were part of a culture that is quite different from ours. They were Eastern (Hebrew) thinkers, while we are Western (Greek) thinkers. Although it is difficult to summarize simply the contrast between ancient Near Eastern thinking and our own, one key difference is our tendency to use abstract definitions and the Israelites' preference to use concrete examples.

Whereas we might define God as omnipotent and compassionate, for example, the Psalmist would say, "The Lord is my shepherd." The image of the shepherd is one of the most profound and common metaphors used in the Bible to describe God and His relationship to His people. The Bible comes alive when we realize that the word pictures it contains, such as the Good Shepherd tending His sheep, are true representations of God's nature and our relationship with Him. The heart of godliness, after all, is relationship, not simply intellectual agreement with truth.

So Ray Vander Laan focuses our attention on the land and people of Israel to help us better understand the Scriptures. For example, he points out that the shepherds who are leading a flock of sheep are children thirteen years of age or younger. Their father—the chief shepherd and head of their Bedouin group—keeps watch from a nearby hill while he handles other responsibilities of wilderness living. In a similar sense, Jesus—whom the Bible calls our "Chief Shepherd"—guides and watches over the "undershepherds"—those who are leaders among His people. Ray then highlights several aspects of Psalm 23.

He reveals how sheep listen to the shepherd's voice but will run away from a stranger's voice, and how sheep follow where their shepherd leads. In a similar way, Jesus—our Good Shepherd—goes in front of us and asks us to follow Him, just as He asked the disciples to follow Him. If we choose to follow Him, He gives us the responsibility of influencing and shaping our culture.

Ray also points out that the grass in the Negev usually isn't very tall, so a shepherd can't take his sheep to green pastures of knee-high grass where they can feast for weeks. Rather, he finds enough pasture to satisfy the flock's need for food today. Although the grass may not be abundant, the sheep don't have to worry about what they will eat later because their shepherd always guides them to new grass when they need it. Likewise, we don't have to worry about what will happen later today, tomorrow, or next week. God wants us to trust Him to provide what we need now—and to meet our needs later. We won't necessarily be led to the green pastures we will need tomorrow until tomorrow comes.

Ray then takes us into a wadi, a usually dry riverbed canyon that can suddenly turn into a torrent of rushing water fed by distant mountain rains, so that we might understand why the Psalmist would say, "God leads me to *quiet* water." Many people try to satisfy their spiritual thirst in potentially dangerous ways. They turn away from the voice of the Good Shepherd, enter the "wadis" in order to find water, and sometimes are swept away by the mountain runoff. They seek to find their own water instead of the good, safe, quiet water that Jesus offers.

At the close of the video, Ray encourages us by pointing out a fairly tall acacia tree growing in a wadi. In the dry Negev, trees and shrubs normally remain small, but in the wadi, trees are nourished by the streams of water that occasionally flow through. Even though the streams are rarely visible, there is sufficient water for the trees to grow tall. Likewise, when we become rooted in God's streams of living water, our lives will show evidence of the nourishment we receive from Him and people will recognize who we are.

## Key Points of This Lesson

1. *Jesus is our Good Shepherd; we are His sheep.* In much the same way that the shepherds of Israel's wilderness lead, protect, and nourish their flocks, Jesus will lead us to green pastures and provide us with what we need for today. He will walk before us, inviting us to follow Him and to model His actions as we interact with other people and influence our culture. He will lead us to quiet water—places of safety where we can be refreshed.

2. Sometimes life is difficult and can be compared to the vast wilderness areas of ancient Israel. Things are parched . . . confusing . . . and dangerous. But *God is our Shepherd—even in the wilderness. In fact, as we learn to trust Him and faithfully follow Him through the wilderness, the roots of our faith will grow strong.*

## Session Outline (52 minutes)

### I. Introduction (5 minutes)
Welcome

What's to Come

Questions to Think About

### II. Show Video "The Lord Is My Shepherd" (16 minutes)

### III. Group Discovery (20 minutes)
Video Highlights

Small Group Bible Discovery

### IV. Faith Lesson (10 minutes)
Time for Reflection

Action Points

### V. Closing Prayer (1 minute)

## Materials

No additional materials are needed for this session. However, you may want to use a marker board, overhead, or chalk board to record participants' answers to the Questions to Think About. Otherwise, simply view the video prior to leading the session so you are familiar with its main points.

# The Lord is my shepherd

## Introduction

5 minutes

### Welcome

Assemble the participants together. Welcome them to session five of *Faith Lessons on the Prophets and Kings of Israel.*

### What's to Come

Perhaps you've seen photographs or videotapes of modern-day shepherds in the Middle East or Africa. Day after day, they guide their sheep away from danger and provide them with necessary food and water. In this video, Ray Vander Laan uses a desert setting to give us new perspectives on the Israelites' wilderness experience—and the many images contained in the Bible that relate to the wilderness. He especially highlights the relationship between a shepherd and his or her sheep. He encourages us to realize that God is, indeed, our Good Shepherd and challenges us to willingly follow and trust Him each day.

### Questions to Think About

*Participant's Guide page 91.*

Ask each question and solicit a few responses from group members. You may want to record participants' responses to these questions on a marker board, chalk board, or overhead. If so, make one list for the first question and another list for the second question. Then compare the lists, pointing out that one is abstract while the other is concrete and visual.

1. Which words would you use to describe the character of God?

   *Suggested Responses:* may include wise, powerful, omniscient, sovereign, just, righteous, holy, etc.

2. Which images or metaphors would you use to complete the sentence: God is like _____?

   *Suggested Responses:* may include such words or phrases as a faithful friend, a shelter, a powerful ruler, living water, a hen gathering her chicks, a vine, a shepherd, etc.

   Let's keep these images in mind as we view the video.

---

**SESSION FIVE**

# The Lord Is My Shepherd

## Questions to Think About

1. Which words would you use to describe the character of God?

2. Which images or metaphors would you use to complete the sentence: God is like _____?

91

---

# video presentation

**16** minutes

*Participant's Guide page 92.*

On page 92 of your Participant's Guide, you will find a space in which to take notes on key points as we watch this video.

### Leader's Video Observations

Discovering the Wilderness

Shepherds and Their Sheep

Jesus—Our Good Shepherd

# Group Discovery

**20** minutes

If your group has seven or more members, use the **Video Highlights** with the entire group (5 minutes), then break into small groups of three to five to discuss the **Small Group Bible Discovery** (10 minutes). Then reassemble the group to discuss the key points discovered (5 minutes).

If your group has fewer than seven members, begin with the **Video Highlights** (5 minutes), then do one or more of the topics found in the **Small Group Bible Discovery** as a group (10 minutes). Finally, spend five minutes at the end discussing points that had an impact on participants.

## video notes

Discovering the Wilderness

Shepherds and Their Sheep

Jesus—Our Good Shepherd

The Judea Wilderness

## Video Highlights (5 minutes)

Here you'll ask one or more of the following questions that directly relate to the video the participants have just seen.

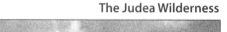

1. Place yourself in the setting of this video. Imagine what it would be like to be a Bedouin shepherd living in the wilderness—no electricity, no running water, no telephone or television, no neighborhood supermarket with its assortment of fresh produce. How might such a lifestyle change your perception of and need for God?

   *Suggested Responses:* Allow participants to share their views. Encourage them to evaluate their need to depend on God's daily provision in such circumstances.

**The Judea Wilderness**

**The Northern Edge of the Wilderness**

## video нighlights

1. Place yourself in the setting of this video. Imagine what it would be like to be a Bedouin shepherd living in the wilderness—no electricity, no running water, no telephone or television, no neighborhood supermarket with its assortment of fresh produce. How might such a lifestyle change your perception of and need for God?

2. In what ways did Ray Vander Laan's explanation of what "green pastures" in the Negev really are surprise you?

**The Northern Edge of the Wilderness**

PLANNING NOTES:

2. In what ways did Ray Vander Laan's explanation of what "green pastures" in the Negev really are surprise you?

*Suggested Responses:* will vary but may include expectations of larger, greener, more abundant pastures.

**Wilderness Pasture**

**Quiet Waters in the Wilderness**

3. What is meant by the term "undershepherd"? In what ways are you an undershepherd who leads other people?

*Suggested Responses:* An undershepherd leads and guides sheep and goats but is accountable to a chief, or more senior, shepherd. The undershepherd also may be a leader of people. Allow participants to share their shepherding roles: teacher, parent, coach, etc.

4. Why is it so dangerous for sheep to drink from water located in wadis? How does this image parallel what people do today to quench their spiritual thirst?

*Suggested Responses:* Water sometimes rushes into wadis (canyons) after rains fall on the distant mountains. Today, some people seek to satisfy their needs in their own way rather than trusting God and looking to Him for their provision. They satisfy their thirst for life in dangerous ways, and they, and their loved ones, may suffer negative consequences.

3. What is meant by the term "undershepherd"? In what ways are you an undershepherd who leads other people?

4. Why is it so dangerous for sheep to drink from water located in wadis? How does this image parallel what people do today to quench their spiritual thirst?

**Wilderness Pasture**     **Quiet Waters in the Wilderness**

## FOR GREATER UNDERSTANDING

### Word Pictures of the Scriptures

The early writers and readers of the Scriptures viewed their world in concrete, not abstract, terms. So they used word pictures and symbolic actions rather than formal definitions to describe God and His relationship with His people. Note what the following word pictures reveal about God and our relationship to Him.

| | |
|---|---|
| John 6:35a | Jesus, the "bread of life," offers spiritual food that will completely satisfy our hunger. He alone offers the spiritual truth that provides life. |
| John 8:12 | Jesus is the "light of the world." He will provide spiritual light for anyone who follows Him, so instead of stumbling in spiritual darkness His followers will be able to follow a clearly lit path. |
| Psalm 18:2 | God is our "rock." He is steadfast, immovable, a sure place on which to stand and take refuge. God is our "fortress," a place of safety. God is our "deliverer" who saves us. He is our "shield" who protects us from harm. He is the "horn," a symbol of strength, of our salvation. |
| Isaiah 40:11 | God is presented as a loving "shepherd." He takes care of His people like a loving shepherd cares for his or her flock. Even the weak and defenseless are secure in His tender care. |
| Psalm 100:3 | God's people are portrayed as the "sheep" of God's pasture, meaning they will receive daily protection and sustenance from Him. |
| John 3:3 | Jesus used the term "born again" to illustrate the spiritual changes that occur when a person accepts Him as Lord and Savior. This word picture reflects the completely new person God creates through His salvation—a person who sees God's kingdom in a new light, a person who has a new hope, new goals, and a new understanding of spiritual truth. |

### FOR GREATER UNDERSTANDING

**Word Pictures of the Scriptures**

The early writers and readers of the Scriptures viewed their world in concrete, not abstract, terms. So they used word pictures and symbolic actions rather than formal definitions to describe God and His relationship with His people. Note what the following word pictures reveal about God and our relationship to Him.

| John 6:35a | Jesus, the "bread of life," offers spiritual food that will completely satisfy our hunger. He alone offers the spiritual truth that provides life. |
| John 8:12 | Jesus is the "light of the world." He will provide spiritual light for anyone who follows Him, so instead of stumbling in spiritual darkness His followers will be able to follow a clearly lit path. |
| Psalm 18:2 | God is our "rock." He is steadfast, immovable, a sure place on which to stand and take refuge. God is our "fortress," a place of safety. God is our "deliverer" who saves us. He is our "shield" who protects us from harm. He is the "horn," a symbol of strength, of our salvation. |
| Isaiah 40:11 | God is presented as a loving "shepherd." He takes care of His people like a loving shepherd cares for his or her flock. Even the weak and defenseless are secure in His tender care. |
| Psalm 100:3 | God's people are portrayed as the "sheep" of God's pasture, meaning they will receive daily protection and sustenance from Him. |
| John 3:3 | Jesus used the term "born again" to illustrate the spiritual changes that occur when a person accepts Him as Lord and Savior. This word picture reflects the completely new person God creates through His salvation—a person who sees God's kingdom in a new light, a person who has a new hope, new goals, and a new understanding of spiritual truth. |

**PLANNING NOTES:**

## Small Group Bible Discovery (15 minutes)

> *Participant's Guide pages 96–107.*
>
> During this time, a group with fewer than seven participants will stay together. A group with seven or more participants will break into small groups and reassemble as a large group during the final five minutes. Assign each group one of the following topics. If you have more than five small groups, assign some topics to more than one group.

Let's break into groups of three to five—people sitting near you—and study some of the Bible passages and truths mentioned in the video.

Turn to pages 96–107 in your Participant's Guide. There you'll find a list of five topics. You'll have ten minutes to read and discuss the topic I'll assign to you. Choose one person in your group to be a spokesperson for your group when we discuss these topics later.

> Assign each group a topic.

I'll signal you when one minute is left.

## Topic A: The Lessons of the Wilderness

The Israelites traversed the wilderness before entering the Promised Land, and their wilderness experience transformed them, as it did a number of leaders of God's people. Let's look at the role the wilderness played in the Israelites' lives.

1. Under what circumstances did Israel's forefathers spend time in the desert before God called them to accomplish His mission for their lives? How did God use these men?

    a. Genesis 12:1–10; 13:1–4

    *Suggested Responses:* God told Abram to leave his home, people, and family and travel to the land He would show him. Abram left, headed through Canaan toward the Negev, and then went into Egypt to escape a famine.

**The Northern Edge of the Wilderness**

## small Group Bible Discovery

**Topic A: The Lessons of the Wilderness**

The Israelites traversed the wilderness before entering the Promised Land, and their wilderness experience transformed them, as it did a number of leaders of God's people. Let's look at the role the wilderness played in the Israelites' lives.

1. Under what circumstances did Israel's forefathers spend time in the desert before God called them to accomplish His mission for their lives? How did God use these men?

   a. Genesis 12:1–10; 13:1–4

   b. Exodus 2:11–22; 3:1–4, 7–10

   c. 1 Samuel 23:12–15; 2 Samuel 2:1–4

The Northern Edge of the Wilderness

Then he and his family went back through the Negev to Bethel, the land that God had promised to give to Abram's descendants.

b.   Exodus 2:11–22; 3:1–4, 7–10

*Suggested Responses:* After Moses killed an Egyptian, he fled to Midian, where he married Zipporah and tended sheep. In the wilderness, while Moses tended the flocks, God revealed Himself in the burning bush and told Moses that he had been chosen to take God's people out of Egypt and lead them to the Promised Land.

c.   1 Samuel 23:12–15; 2 Samuel 2:1–4

*Suggested Response:* Pursued by King Saul, who wanted to kill him, David and his men fled into the safety of the desert wilderness. Later, after Saul died, David became king of Judah and all of Israel.

2.   Biblical writers understood that while His people were in the desert, God nurtured and disciplined them so they would learn to depend solely on Him. Read Psalm 78:12–29 and note what God did to nurture their faith in Him.

*Suggested Responses:* God divided the sea and led them through it, guided them with a cloud by day and a fire by night, and gave them abundant water from a rock. Even with this provision, the Israelites challenged God's ability to provide for them. So God became angry with them for not believing in Him and not trusting in His ability to provide. Yet He patiently "opened the doors of the heavens" and gave them the bread of angels (manna) and provided an abundance of meat. In spite of what God did, however, they kept on sinning and did not believe in Him.

3.   Of what did King David remind the Israelites? Which images did he use to make his point? (See Psalm 95:6–11.)

*Suggested Response:* David urged the people to bow down before God. Using the imagery of a shepherd and his sheep, David reminded the Israelites that they were the people of God's pasture—the flock under God's care—and warned them not to test God again by hardening their hearts and disbelieving His miraculous provision.

4.   Through the prophetic words of Jeremiah, what did God say to the Israelites in Canaan? (See Jeremiah 2:1–7.)

*Suggested Responses:* God reminded the Israelites of their ancestors' loyalty to Him in the wilderness. He asked, with a sense of painful longing, why their fathers had followed idols and not turned to Him, even after He had led them through the barren wilderness and guided them to the fertile land of Canaan.

5.   What did God, through Moses, say to the people as they were preparing to enter the Promised Land? (See Deuteronomy 8:1–6, 10–18.)

*Suggested Responses:* God told the Israelites to obey all of His commands, to remember how He had led them through the wilderness in order to humble them and test their determination to follow Him. He said that He had disciplined them as a father disciplines his son, but had kept their clothing and feet in good shape. God also warned them not to become complacent when they became satisfied and wealthy, to remember what He had done for them in the wilderness, and to remember that He—not they—had enabled them to become wealthy.

2. Biblical writers understood that while His people were in the desert, God nurtured and disciplined them so they would learn to depend solely on Him. Read Psalm 78:12–29 and note what God did to nurture their faith in Him.

3. Of what did King David remind the Israelites? Which images did he use to make his point? (See Psalm 95:6–11.)

4. Through the prophetic words of Jeremiah, what did God say to the Israelites in Canaan? (See Jeremiah 2:1–7.)

5. What did God, through Moses, say to the people as they were preparing to enter the Promised Land? (See Deuteronomy 8:1–6, 10–18.)

## DATA FILE

### The Wilderness of Israel

Much of Israel is rugged desert. The two most significant wilderness areas in Israel are the Judea Wilderness to the east and the Negev to the south. These deserts contain more rock than sand, are mountainous in spots, and receive just enough rainfall during winter months to sustain nomadic shepherds and their flocks.

#### The Judea Wilderness

The Judea Mountains form the middle section of the central mountain range in Israel. On the eastern side of this mountain ridge, descending into the Great Rift Valley more than 1,300 feet below sea level, is the rocky wasteland of Judah. Little rain falls here, and the land is split by deep wadis formed by centuries of rain runoff. Because this wilderness borders fertile mountain ridges for more than fifty miles, villages such as Bethlehem were able to sustain both shepherds (like David) and farmers (like Boaz and Ruth). Shepherds lived on the desert's fringes; farmers worked the soil of the mountains.

#### The Negev

The arid Negev (*Negev* means "dry") lies south of the Hebron Mountains that form the southern section of Israel's central mountain range. This desert receives fewer than eight inches of rainfall annually in the north and less than half that amount in the south. Except for a few settlements that use modern methods to catch rain runoff, only nomads live here.

Because the wilderness was so close to settled areas, many people seeking solitude or safety from authorities hid there. For example, in the Negev David hid from Saul (1 Samuel 26), John the Baptist isolated himself from religious practices of the day (Matthew 3), and Jesus faced the devil (Matthew 4). People also associated the wilderness with the coming of the Messiah. Isaiah 40:3b reads, "In the desert prepare the way for the LORD; make straight in the wilderness a highway for our God."

The northern region of the Negev, from the Hebron Mountains to the Zin Wilderness, is good sheep country. Its rolling hills surround large, broad valleys such as the Valley of Beersheba in which Abraham settled. The Negev's central region is rugged and cut by deep canyons in the Zin Wilderness. Because the climate and terrain are so inhospitable—even to nomads—at least one scholar has suggested that the "valley of the shadow of death" mentioned in Psalm 23 may refer to the canyons here. The southern portion of the Negev is called the Wilderness of Paran in the Bible. This region is the most barren of all.

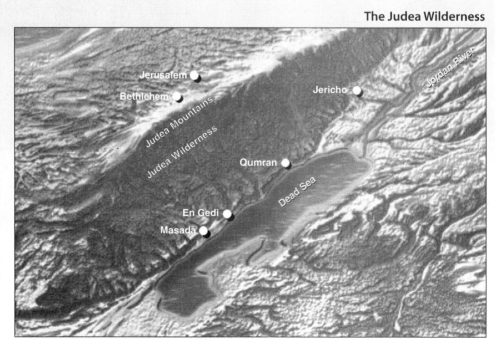

**The Judea Wilderness**

## DATA FILE

### The Wilderness of Israel

Much of Israel is rugged desert. The two most significant wilderness areas in Israel are the Judea Wilderness to the east and the Negev to the south. These deserts contain more rock than sand, are mountainous in spots, and receive just enough rainfall during winter months to sustain nomadic shepherds and their flocks.

#### The Judea Wilderness

The Judea Mountains form the middle section of the central mountain range in Israel. On the eastern side of this mountain ridge, descending into the Great Rift Valley more than 1,300 feet below sea level, is the rocky wasteland of Judah. Little rain falls here, and the land is split by deep wadis formed by centuries of rain runoff. Because this wilderness borders fertile mountain ridges for more than fifty miles, villages such as Bethlehem were able to sustain both shepherds (like David) and farmers (like Boaz and Ruth). Shepherds lived on the desert's fringes; farmers worked the soil of the mountains.

#### The Negev

The arid Negev (*Negev* means "dry") lies south of the Hebron Mountains that form the southern section of Israel's central mountain range. This desert receives fewer than eight inches of rainfall annually in the north and less than half that amount in the south. Except for a few settlements that use modern methods to catch rain runoff, only nomads live here.

Because the wilderness was so close to settled areas, many people seeking solitude or safety from authorities hid there. For example, in the Negev David hid from Saul (1 Samuel 26), John the Baptist isolated himself from religious practices of the day (Matthew 3), and Jesus faced the devil (Matthew 4). People also associated the wilderness with the coming of the Messiah. Isaiah 40:3b reads, "In the desert prepare the way for the Lord; make straight in the wilderness a highway for our God."

The northern region of the Negev, from the Hebron Mountains to the Zin Wilderness, is good sheep country. Its rolling hills surround large, broad valleys such as the Valley of Beersheba in which Abraham settled.

The Negev's central region is rugged and cut by deep canyons in the Zin Wilderness. Because the climate and terrain are so inhospitable—even to nomads—at least one scholar has suggested that the "valley of the shadow of death" mentioned in Psalm 23 may refer to the canyons here. The southern portion of the Negev is called the Wilderness of Paran in the Bible. This region is the most barren of all.

**The Judea Wilderness**

### Topic B: "The Shepherd"

The shepherd image appears more than 200 times in the Bible, including more than 15 times in the New Testament. Knowing that the Israelites, as shepherds, would clearly understand the relationship of the shepherd and his sheep, God used it to illustrate His relationship with His people.

✏ 1. What do the images of the shepherd and his sheep in the following verses reveal about God and His people?

a. Isaiah 40:10–11

*Suggested Responses:* The sovereign God cares for His flock like a shepherd. God gathers up and carries the lambs (those who are weak, helpless, young) and leads those who have young (those who are vulnerable).

b. Psalm 95:6–7

*Suggested Response:* God is our God and we are the flock under His care.

c. Psalm 78:51–54

*Suggested Response:* The Psalmist compared the Israelites' miraculous exodus from Egypt to a flock of sheep being led safely through the desert, through the Red Sea, and into the Shepherd's "holy land" (Canaan).

d. Psalm 100:3

*Suggested Response:* The Psalmist wrote that we are the "sheep" of God's pasture.

e. Luke 12:22–32

*Suggested Response:* Jesus calmed the anxious fears of His disciples. He explained how God cares for the ravens, the lilies, and the grass, and how much more He will provide for the needs of His people. Then He tenderly admonished His "little flock" to not be afraid, because the heavenly Father (by implication, the Good Shepherd) wanted to abundantly provide for them.

f. Luke 15:3–7

*Suggested Response:* Jesus' parable illustrates the value of each "lost sheep," each sinner. Jesus shared how a shepherd will search for one lost sheep until he finds it, and then will rejoice with his friends that it was found. Likewise, all of heaven rejoices when one sinner repents.

g. John 10:14–16

*Suggested Responses:* Jesus said that He was the Good Shepherd, who cared so much for His sheep that He would lay down His life for them. He talked about the need for Him to bring in other sheep, too, who will listen to His voice. He also talked about a time when there will be "one flock" and "one shepherd."

**Topic B: "The Shepherd"**

The shepherd image appears more than 200 times in the Bible, including more than 15 times in the New Testament. Knowing that the Israelites, as shepherds, would clearly understand the relationship of the shepherd and his sheep, God used it to illustrate His relationship with His people.

1. What do the images of the shepherd and his sheep in the following verses reveal about God and His people?

   Isaiah 40:10–11

   Psalm 95:6–7

   Psalm 78:51–54

   Psalm 100:3

   Luke 12:22–32

   Luke 15:3–7

   John 10:14–16

**FACTS TO PONDER**

**The Myth of Green Pastures**

Although we might think that the "green pastures" David mentioned in Psalm 23 refer to tall, lush grasslands like those in North America and other locations, the truth is that such grasslands don't exist in Israel. The regions in Israel where shepherds live have two seasons: the rainy season from November through March (when even the desert becomes green), and the dry season from April through October when the landscape is brown. Even during the rainy season, the grasses remain short. Sheep that graze in the marginal areas of the wilderness receive enough nourishment for the moment . . . but no more. Day to day, the sheep depend on their shepherd to lead them to the food and water they need.

In Exodus 16:4–5, 13–18, we read that God—the Good Shepherd—provided bread and quail from heaven for His people every day. The Israelites were to take what they needed for that day . . . and no more. But some people took too much to make sure they'd have some the next day (Exodus 16:20). When that happened, the food they tried to store became full of maggots and smelled awful.

Knowing that each of us has the tendency to worry about the future, Jesus shared how important it is for us to trust God to meet our needs every day. He taught that we should seek God and His righteousness and trust Him to meet our needs today . . . and then to trust Him tomorrow in the same way. "Therefore," He said, "do not worry about tomorrow" (Matthew 6:34; see also 6:25–33).

## Topic C: A Promise Made in the Wilderness

Because of our sinful nature, we often pursue our desires instead of God's will. But God is patient and faithful. When we fail to do His bidding, God often provides another opportunity to obey Him and fulfill His plan. Consider how God used the Israelites' experience with the Amalekites to teach His people the crucial importance of obedience.

✏ 1.   What did the Amalekites do, and what did God promise to do to them? (See Exodus 17:8–14.)

*Suggested Response:* The nomadic Amalekites attacked the Israelites during the exodus from Egypt, but God miraculously allowed the Israelites to conquer them. Then God promised to completely remove the memory of Amalek from the earth.

✏ 2.   What did God command the Israelites to do? (See Deuteronomy 25:17–19.)

*Suggested Response:* God told them to remember how the Amalekites had killed the weary Israelite stragglers during the exodus from Egypt. When the Israelites were at peace in Canaan, they were to blot out Amalek's memory.

## FACTS TO PONDER

### The Myth of Green Pastures

Although we might think that the "green pastures" David mentioned in Psalm 23 refer to tall, lush grasslands like those in North America and other locations, the truth is that such grasslands don't exist in Israel. The regions in Israel where shepherds live have two seasons: the rainy season from November through March (when even the desert becomes green), and the dry season from April through October when the landscape is brown. Even during the rainy season, the grasses remain short. Sheep that graze in the marginal areas of the wilderness receive enough nourishment for the moment . . . but no more. Day to day, the sheep depend on their shepherd to lead them to the food and water they need.

In Exodus 16:4–5, 13–18, we read that God—the Good Shepherd—provided bread and quail from heaven for His people every day. The Israelites were to take what they needed for that day . . . and no more. But some people took too much to make sure they'd have some the next day (Exodus 16:20). When that happened, the food they tried to store became full of maggots and smelled awful.

Knowing that each of us has the tendency to worry about the future, Jesus shared how important it is for us to trust God to meet our needs every day. He taught that we should seek God and His righteousness and trust Him to meet our needs today . . . and then to trust Him tomorrow in the same way. "Therefore," He said, "do not worry about tomorrow" (Matthew 6:34; see also 6:25–33).

### Topic C: A Promise Made in the Wilderness

Because of our sinful nature, we often pursue our desires instead of God's will. But God is patient and faithful. When we fail to do His bidding, God often provides another opportunity to obey Him and fulfill His plan. Consider how God used the Israelites' experience with the Amalekites to teach His people the crucial importance of obedience.

1. What did the Amalekites do, and what did God promise to do to them? (See Exodus 17:8–14.)

2. What did God command the Israelites to do? (See Deuteronomy 25:17–19.)

3. What did God, through Samuel, tell King Saul to do? (See 1 Samuel 15:1–4.)

4. What did King Saul do in response to God's command? (See 1 Samuel 15:7–9, 20–25.) What was God's response?

5. About 400 years after Saul's disobedience and death, how did a descendant of Agag, Haman, endanger the entire nation of Israel? (See Esther 3:1–6, 8–11.)

PLANNING NOTES:

## PROFILE OF A PEOPLE

### The Israelites in the Wilderness

After God miraculously delivered the Israelites from Egyptian bondage, they wandered through the Negev and the Sinai Wilderness. When they reached the northern edge of the Negev, the Israelites sent spies into Canaan. Upon learning about giants and huge fortified cities, the people became afraid and refused to enter the Promised Land. Because of their disobedience and lack of faith, God commanded them to remain in the wilderness—"the vast and dreadful desert" (Deuteronomy 8:15)—for forty years, one year for each day the spies had been gone.

During these desert years, God taught His people faith and trust, preparing them to live obediently in the Promised Land *so that the world would know that He was God.* He also disciplined them for their lack of faith, disobedience, and complaining. Moses recorded that God humbled the Israelites so that they would learn to depend on Him for everything, because "man does not live on bread alone but on every word that comes from the mouth of the LORD" (Deuteronomy 8:3).

For obvious reasons, their forty-year wilderness wanderings significantly impacted the Israelites. Various Bible references emphasize the lessons they learned:

- The Psalmist reminded the Israelites of God's faithful love in the wilderness (Psalm 105:38–45; 107:4–9).
- The Psalmist warned the Israelites against repeating their earlier sins (Psalm 81:11–16; 78:14–40).
- Jeremiah reminded the Israelites of what God had done for them and how they had disobeyed Him and disregarded His warnings (Jeremiah 2:5–8; 7:21–26).
- Micah reminded them of God's previous blessings (Micah 6:3–5).
- The writer of Hebrews used the Israelites' wilderness wandering as an illustration of unbelief (Hebrews 3:7–19).
- Paul summarized some of the Israelites' sins in the wilderness and reminded readers to be careful (1 Corinthians 10:1–13).
- Jesus, when He faced the tempter, used the lessons of the wilderness to defeat him. (See Matthew 4:4 and Deuteronomy 8:3; Matthew 4:7 and Deuteronomy 6:16.)

Today, the wilderness imagery of the Bible refers to our lives here on earth as we prepare for our "promised land" in heaven. It portrays difficult times in our lives when we learn to trust God. It offers a picture of God disciplining us for our sins and reminds us of the Messiah's eventual return. Truly the wilderness is still the place where we—God's people—learn that we cannot live on bread alone.

### PROFILE OF A PEOPLE

**The Israelites in the Wilderness**

After God miraculously delivered the Israelites from Egyptian bondage, they wandered through the Negev and the Sinai Wilderness. When they reached the northern edge of the Negev, the Israelites sent spies into Canaan. Upon learning about giants and huge fortified cities, the people became afraid and refused to enter the Promised Land. Because of their disobedience and lack of faith, God commanded them to remain in the wilderness—"the vast and dreadful desert" (Deuteronomy 8:15)—for forty years, one year for each day the spies had been gone.

During these desert years, God taught His people faith and trust, preparing them to live obediently in the Promised Land *so that the world would know that He was God.* He also disciplined them for their lack of faith, disobedience, and complaining. Moses recorded that God humbled the Israelites so that they would learn to depend on Him for everything, because "man does not live on bread alone but on every word that comes from the mouth of the LORD" (Deuteronomy 8:3).

For obvious reasons, their forty-year wilderness wanderings significantly impacted the Israelites. Various Bible references emphasize the lessons they learned:

- The Psalmist reminded the Israelites of God's faithful love in the wilderness (Psalm 105:38–45; 107:4–9).
- The Psalmist warned the Israelites against repeating their earlier sins (Psalm 81:11–16; 78:14–40).
- Jeremiah reminded the Israelites of what God had done for them and how they had disobeyed Him and disregarded His warnings (Jeremiah 2:5–8; 7:21–26).
- Micah reminded them of God's previous blessings (Micah 6:3–5).
- The writer of Hebrews used the Israelites' wilderness wandering as an illustration of unbelief (Hebrews 3:7–19).
- Paul summarized some of the Israelites' sins in the wilderness and reminded readers to be careful (1 Corinthians 10:1–13).

(continued on page 104)

(continued from page 103)

- Jesus, when He faced the tempter, used the lessons of the wilderness to defeat him. (See Matthew 4:4 and Deuteronomy 8:3; Matthew 4:7 and Deuteronomy 6:16.)

Today, the wilderness imagery of the Bible refers to our lives here on earth as we prepare for our "promised land" in heaven. It portrays difficult times in our lives when we learn to trust God. It offers a picture of God disciplining us for our sins and reminds us of the Messiah's eventual return. Truly the wilderness is still the place where we—God's people—learn that we cannot live on bread alone.

6. What opportunity did God, in His mercy, give to Esther, a descendant of Kish, Saul's father? (See 1 Samuel 9:1–2; Esther 2:5–11, 16–17; 4:12–17; 7:1–6, 9–10.)

7. How do the prophetic words of Mordecai, Esther's uncle, relate to what God may be calling us to do and be in our unique circumstances? (See Esther 4:12–16.)

## PLANNING NOTES:

✐ 3.  What did God, through Samuel, tell King Saul to do? (See 1 Samuel 15:1–4.)

*Suggested Response:* When Samuel anointed Saul as king, he said that God wanted King Saul to attack the Amalekites and to completely destroy everything that belonged to them.

✐ 4.  What did King Saul do in response to God's command? (See 1 Samuel 15:7–9, 20–25.) What was God's response?

*Suggested Response:* Saul disobeyed God by sparing Agag—the Amalekite king—and the best of the Amalekites' animals. Thus, like Achan (Joshua 7), Saul attempted to keep for himself what God had forbidden. God then rejected Saul as king.

✐ 5.  About 400 years after Saul's disobedience and death, how did a descendant of Agag, Haman, endanger the entire nation of Israel? (See Esther 3:1–6, 8–11.)

*Suggested Response:* Haman determined to destroy all the Jews throughout the kingdom of Xerxes, the Persian ruler. Haman then convinced Xerxes to issue a decree (that could not be changed) stating that all the Jews were to be killed.

✐ 6.  What opportunity did God, in His mercy, give to Esther, a descendant of Kish, Saul's father? (See 1 Samuel 9:1–2; Esther 2:5–11, 16–17; 4:12–17; 7:1–6, 9–10.)

*Suggested Responses:* Esther had become Xerxes' queen. When Mordecai learned about Haman's plot to kill all the Jews in Persia, he communicated to Esther that God may well have placed her in her royal position to deliver the Jews from Haman's plot. So despite the risk to her life, she asked the king to hear her request. She invited the king and Haman to a banquet at which she revealed Haman's plot to kill her people. The king then put Haman to death. Thus a descendant of Saul's father had the opportunity to fulfill the promise Saul had broken—to destroy Agag's family.

✐ 7.  How do the prophetic words of Mordecai, Esther's uncle, relate to what God may be calling us to do and be in our unique circumstances? (See Esther 4:12–16.)

*Suggested Responses:* Like Esther, each of us must consider how God may have placed us in unique circumstances for the purpose of serving His kingdom. Our faithfulness may produce blessings for generations after we are gone from this earth.

**Topic C: A Promise Made in the Wilderness**

Because of our sinful nature, we often pursue our desires instead of God's will. But God is patient and faithful. When we fail to do His bidding, God often provides another opportunity to obey Him and fulfill His plan. Consider how God used the Israelites' experience with the Amalekites to teach His people the crucial importance of obedience.

1. What did the Amalekites do, and what did God promise to do to them? (See Exodus 17:8–14.)

2. What did God command the Israelites to do? (See Deuteronomy 25:17–19.)

3. What did God, through Samuel, tell King Saul to do? (See 1 Samuel 15:1–4.)

4. What did King Saul do in response to God's command? (See 1 Samuel 15:7–9, 20–25.) What was God's response?

5. About 400 years after Saul's disobedience and death, how did a descendant of Agag, Haman, endanger the entire nation of Israel? (See Esther 3:1–6, 8–11.)

(continued from page 103)

• Jesus, when He faced the tempter, used the lessons of the wilderness to defeat him. (See Matthew 4:4 and Deuteronomy 8:3; Matthew 4:7 and Deuteronomy 6:16.)

Today, the wilderness imagery of the Bible refers to our lives here on earth as we prepare for our "promised land" in heaven. It portrays difficult times in our lives when we learn to trust God. It offers a picture of God disciplining us for our sins and reminds us of the Messiah's eventual return. Truly the wilderness is still the place where we—God's people—learn that we cannot live on bread alone.

6. What opportunity did God, in His mercy, give to Esther, a descendant of Kish, Saul's father? (See 1 Samuel 9:1–2; Esther 2:5–11, 16–17; 4:12–17; 7:1–6, 9–10.)

7. How do the prophetic words of Mordecai, Esther's uncle, relate to what God may be calling us to do and be in our unique circumstances? (See Esther 4:12–16.)

PLANNING NOTES:

## Topic D: Undershepherds

Some scholars believe that the practice of young shepherds tending sheep under the watchful eyes of adults is the basis for the biblical picture of God—the Chief Shepherd—appointing undershepherds to care for His flock.

1. What does 1 Samuel 16:10–13 reveal about the son of Jesse whom God had chosen to be king of Israel?

   *Suggested Response:* We learn that David, the youngest of eight sons of Jesse, was not even considered when Samuel came to anoint the next king of Israel. David was caring for the sheep.

2. What happened to the undershepherds who cared for their father's flock in Midian? (See Exodus 2:16–17.)

   *Suggested Response:* The seven daughters were trying to fill the troughs with water for their father's flock when other shepherds came and drove away the girls. But Moses helped them and watered their flock for them.

3. What terminology did Jesus use to give Peter the responsibility to care for His flock? (See John 21:15–17.)

   *Suggested Response:* Because Peter said that he loved Jesus, Jesus told him to "feed my lambs," "take care of my sheep," and "feed my sheep."

4. Whom did God condemn in Ezekiel 34:1–10? Why? What imagery did God use to make His point?

   *Suggested Response:* God strongly condemned the "shepherds of Israel" who had not taken care of God's flock. They did not strengthen the weak, heal the sick, bind up the injured, bring back the scattered, or seek the lost. Instead, the shepherds had oppressed the flock and cared for themselves. As a result, God's flock had been plundered and preyed upon, so God promised to rescue his sheep.

5. After the undershepherds of Israel failed in their God-given responsibilities, what did God promise to do? (See Ezekiel 34:11–16.)

   *Suggested Responses:* God promised to search for His sheep, deliver them, and care for them Himself. He said that He would unite them in their own land, pasture them in good places, and give them rest.

6. What imagery did Paul use when speaking to the Ephesian elders, and what did he tell them to do? (See Acts 20:28–31.)

   *Suggested Responses:* Paul used the imagery of shepherding. He told them to watch out for themselves and for the flock over which God had placed them. He urged them to shepherd the church of God and to be on guard against the "wolves" that would come into the flock and harm its members.

7. What did God promise to do to the shepherds who had not cared for the sheep He had entrusted to them? (See Jeremiah 23:1–4.) And what did He promise to do for the sheep?

**Topic D: Undershepherds**

Some scholars believe that the practice of young shepherds tending sheep under the watchful eyes of adults is the basis for the biblical picture of God—the Chief Shepherd—appointing undershepherds to care for His flock.

1. What does 1 Samuel 16:10–13 reveal about the son of Jesse whom God had chosen to be king of Israel?

2. What happened to the undershepherds who cared for their father's flock in Midian? (See Exodus 2:16–17.)

3. What terminology did Jesus use to give Peter the responsibility to care for His flock? (See John 21:15–17.)

4. Whom did God condemn in Ezekiel 34:1–10? Why? What imagery did God use to make His point?

5. After the undershepherds of Israel failed in their God-given responsibilities, what did God promise to do? (See Ezekiel 34:11–16.)

6. What imagery did Paul use when speaking to the Ephesian elders, and what did he tell them to do? (See Acts 20:28–31.)

7. What did God promise to do to the shepherds who had not cared for the sheep He had entrusted to them? (See Jeremiah 23:1–4.) And what did He promise to do for the sheep?

8. What guidelines did God, through Peter's writing, give to undershepherds who cared for His people? What did God promise would happen when Jesus—the "Chief Shepherd"—appears? (See 1 Peter 5:2–4.)

*Suggested Responses:* God condemned the shepherds who were destroying and scattering His people and promised to punish those shepherds. Then, God promised to gather His people from many places and place them into "their pasture" where they would be fruitful. He also promised to give His people new shepherds who would care for them properly.

8. What guidelines did God, through Peter's writing, give to undershepherds who cared for His people? What did God promise would happen when Jesus—the "Chief Shepherd"—appears? (See 1 Peter 5:2–4.)

*Suggested Response:* The undershepherds were to care for God's flock willingly, eagerly serving and being godly examples that the people could follow. When Jesus appears, the undershepherds will receive "the crown of glory."

## Topic E: The Chief Shepherd—Committed to Leading His Sheep

1. Whereas shepherds in the Western world use dogs to drive their sheep ahead of them, shepherds in the Middle East *lead* their sheep. Look up the following Scriptures and discover how God led the Israelites out of Egypt.

Psalm 78:51–53

*Suggested Response:* In leading the Israelites out of Egypt, God led them as a shepherd would have led sheep. He guided them safely through the desert, so they were unafraid.

Exodus 13:20–22

*Suggested Response:* God "went ahead of them" (walked ahead of them) and provided a pillar of cloud to guide them by day and a pillar of fire to guide them by night.

2. As a result of God's leadership, what would the Israelites receive? (See Isaiah 49:8–10.)

*Suggested Response:* The Israelites would receive God's help. He would care for them, providing plenty to eat and drink during their journey—even in the barren places. He also had compassion on them and would protect them from the sun and heat and guide them to springs of water.

3. To what did Jesus compare His relationship to His followers? What sacrifice was He willing to make for them? (See John 10:11–14.)

*Suggested Response:* Jesus compared His relationship to that of a shepherd leading his or her sheep. Because He was a shepherd who loved His sheep, He was willing to die so that His sheep could be saved.

4. What does Matthew 18:12–14 reveal about God the Shepherd and His commitment to His sheep?

*Suggested Responses:* Every one of His sheep is valuable to Him. When one wanders off on a confusing path and becomes lost, He will seek it out and will rejoice greatly when it is safely returned to the fold. He does not want even one to perish.

106                     Faith Lessons on the Prophets and Kings of Israel

5. After the undershepherds of Israel failed in their God-given responsibilities, what did God promise to do? (See Ezekiel 34:11–16.)

6. What imagery did Paul use when speaking to the Ephesian elders, and what did he tell them to do? (See Acts 20:28–31.)

7. What did God promise to do to the shepherds who had not cared for the sheep He had entrusted to them? (See Jeremiah 23:1–4.) And what did He promise to do for the sheep?

8. What guidelines did God, through Peter's writing, give to undershepherds who cared for His people? What did God promise would happen when Jesus—the "Chief Shepherd"—appears? (See 1 Peter 5:2–4.)

Session Five: The Lord Is My Shepherd                           107

**Topic E: The Chief Shepherd—Committed to Leading His Sheep**

1. Whereas shepherds in the Western world use dogs to drive their sheep ahead of them, shepherds in the Middle East *lead* their sheep. Look up the following Scriptures and discover how God led the Israelites out of Egypt.

Psalm 78:51–53

Exodus 13:20–22

2. As a result of God's leadership, what would the Israelites receive? (See Isaiah 49:8–10.)

3. To what did Jesus compare His relationship to His followers? What sacrifice was He willing to make for them? (See John 10:11–14.)

4. What does Matthew 18:12–14 reveal about God the Shepherd and His commitment to His sheep?

5. How did God use the imagery of sheep to communicate what had happened to His people? (See Jeremiah 50:6, 17–19.)

PLANNING NOTES:

✏ 5.  How did God use the imagery of sheep to communicate what had happened to His people? (See Jeremiah 50:6, 17–19.)

*Suggested Response:* God said, through the prophet Jeremiah, that the shepherds of His people had led the sheep astray. Consequently His people had wandered and forgotten their place of rest and safety. So predators devoured them. As their Shepherd, the Lord promised to punish those who devoured His people and would one day bring His flock back to the pastures that would satisfy them.

> After nine minutes, let participants know that they have one minute remaining. Then reassemble the entire group. After everyone is back together, begin asking one person from each small group to briefly share a key idea with the larger group. In some cases, you may not have time for every group to share their discoveries.

As time allows, let's briefly share the key ideas that your group discussed.

## DATA FILE

### The Wadis of Israel

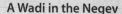
**A Wadi in the Negev**

The wilderness of Israel is scarred by deep, riverbed canyons called *wadis* (Hebrew, *nahal*). Although the wilderness in Israel receives little rainfall, the central mountains receive a great deal of moisture during the winter months. The thin topsoil of the mountains cannot absorb all this water, which runs into the valleys to the west and runs through the wadis into the desert wilderness areas that lie to the east and south.

The runoff is so great that the wadis quickly fill with raging torrents. The water rushes down and roars through the wadis, cutting deep walls into

**Flood in the Wadi**

them and sweeping away any animals or people in its path. These flash floods can occur even when the sky is clear because the rains fall some distance away. Even today, these floods pose a great danger to shepherds and their sheep.

Wadis both hinder and help the shepherds. On one hand, crossing the wadis is difficult and can be very dangerous. Sheep, which are undiscerning, will choose to walk in dangerous water. That's why the shepherd must *lead* the sheep. But the flash floods that crash through the dry canyons leave behind quiet, refreshing pools that enable vegetation to grow and provide watering places for sheep. It is the shepherd's task to determine if these pools are safe for the flock to drink from and lie beside—if they are the "quiet waters" referred to in Psalm 23:2.

**Topic E: The Chief Shepherd—Committed to Leading His Sheep**

1. Whereas shepherds in the Western world use dogs to drive their sheep ahead of them, shepherds in the Middle East *lead* their sheep. Look up the following Scriptures and discover how God led the Israelites out of Egypt.

   Psalm 78:51–53

   Exodus 13:20–22

2. As a result of God's leadership, what would the Israelites receive? (See Isaiah 49:8–10.)

3. To what did Jesus compare His relationship to His followers? What sacrifice was He willing to make for them? (See John 10:11–14.)

4. What does Matthew 18:12–14 reveal about God the Shepherd and His commitment to His sheep?

5. How did God use the imagery of sheep to communicate what had happened to His people? (See Jeremiah 50:6, 17–19.)

**DATA FILE**

**The Wadis of Israel**

The wilderness of Israel is scarred by deep, riverbed canyons called *wadis* (Hebrew, *nahal*). Although the wilderness in Israel receives little rainfall, the central mountains receive a great deal of moisture during the winter months. The thin topsoil of the mountains cannot absorb all this water, which runs into the valleys to the west and runs through the wadis into the desert wilderness areas that lie to the east and south.

The runoff is so great that the wadis quickly fill with raging torrents. The water rushes down and roars through the wadis, cutting deep walls into them and sweeping away any animals or people in its path. These flash floods can occur even when the sky is clear because the rains fall some distance away. Even today, these floods pose a great danger to shepherds and their sheep.

Wadis both hinder and help the shepherds. On one hand, crossing the wadis is difficult and can be very dangerous. Sheep, which are undiscerning, will choose to walk in dangerous water. That's why the shepherd

| A Wadi in the Negev | Flood in the Wadi |
|---|---|

# faith Lesson

## Time for Reflection (7 minutes)

On page 109 of the Participant's Guide, you'll find a passage of Scripture. Let's each read this passage silently and take the next few minutes to consider some of the questions that follow the Scripture passage.

Please do not talk during this time. It's a time when we all can reflect on the significance of the wilderness and the role of the Good Shepherd in our lives today.

*The Scripture passage and questions are reproduced in their entirety in the Participant's Guide on pages 109–112.*

> The LORD is my shepherd, I shall not be in want.
> He makes me lie down in green pastures,
> he leads me beside quiet waters,
> he restores my soul.
> He guides me in paths of righteousness
> for his name's sake.
> Even though I walk
> through the valley of the shadow of death,
> I will fear no evil, for you are with me;
> your rod and your staff, they comfort me.
> You prepare a table before me
> in the presence of my enemies.
> You anoint my head with oil;
> my cup overflows.
> Surely goodness and love will follow me
> all the days of my life,
> and I will dwell in the house of the LORD
> forever.
>
> PSALM 23

1.  What brought hope to the Psalmist as he faced the challenges of his life?

2.  What brings hope to your life?

3.  In light of what you learned in this session about what the "green pastures" in Israel are really like, how do you view the provision God gives you *today* and what He promises to provide for you *tomorrow*?

This psalm is so familiar that it's easy to overlook the profound message it expresses. Take a few minutes to meditate on this psalm and personalize it:

- What does your Shepherd provide for you so that you do not want?
- What are the green pastures and quiet waters of your life?
- In what ways does He restore your soul?
- Identify the paths of righteousness into which He leads you for *His* sake.

must *lead* the sheep. But the flash floods that crash through the dry canyons leave behind quiet, refreshing pools that enable vegetation to grow and provide watering places for sheep. It is the shepherd's task to determine if these pools are safe for the flock to drink from and lie beside—if they are the "quiet waters" referred to in Psalm 23:2.

## faith Lesson

### Time for Reflection

Read the following passage of Scripture and take the next few minutes to reflect on the significance of the wilderness and the role of the Good Shepherd in your life.

> The LORD is my shepherd, I shall not be in want.
> He makes me lie down in green pastures,
> he leads me beside quiet waters,
> he restores my soul.
> He guides me in paths of righteousness
> for his name's sake.
> Even though I walk
> through the valley of the shadow of death,
> I will fear no evil, for you are with me;
> your rod and your staff, they comfort me.
> You prepare a table before me
> in the presence of my enemies.
> You anoint my head with oil;
> my cup overflows.
> Surely goodness and love will follow me
> all the days of my life,
> and I will dwell in the house of the LORD
> forever.
>
> PSALM 23

1. What brought hope to the psalmist as he faced the challenges of his life?

2. What brings hope to your life?

3. In light of what you learned in this session about what the "green pastures" in Israel are really like, how do you view the provision God gives you *today* and what He promises to provide for you *tomorrow*?

**Water from Rock**

- What is the valley of the shadow of death that strikes fear into your heart?
- In what ways does God comfort you?
- Describe the feast He has prepared for you in the sight of your enemies.
- How have you felt His anointing?
- In what ways does your cup overflow?
- What assurance do you have that you will dwell in the house of the Lord forever?

**Water from Rock**

## Action Points (3 minutes)

> *The following points are reproduced on pages 113–114 of the Participant's Guide:*

Now it's time to wrap up our session.

> **Give participants a moment to transition from their thoughtfulness to giving you their full attention.**

I'd like to take a moment to summarize the key points we explored. After I have reviewed these points, I will give you a moment to jot down an action step (or steps) that you will commit to this week as a result of what you have learned today.

> **Read the following points and pause after each so that participants can consider and write out their commitment.**

Session Five: The Lord Is My Shepherd                    111

This psalm is so familiar that it's easy to overlook the profound message it expresses. Take a few minutes to meditate on this psalm and personalize it:

1. What does your Shepherd provide for you so that you do not want?

2. What are the green pastures and quiet waters of your life?

3. In what ways does He restore your soul?

4. Identify the paths of righteousness into which He leads you for *His* sake.

5. What is the valley of the shadow of death that strikes fear into your heart?

112                 Faith Lessons on the Prophets and Kings of Israel

6. In what ways does God comfort you?

7. Describe the feast He has prepared for you in the sight of your enemies.

8. How have you felt His anointing?

9. In what ways does your cup overflow?

10. What assurance do you have that you will dwell in the house of the Lord forever?

PLANNING NOTES:

1.   *Jesus is our Good Shepherd; we are His sheep.* In much the same way that the shepherds of Israel's wilderness lead, protect, and nourish their flocks, Jesus will lead us to green pastures and provide us with what we need for today. He will walk before us, inviting us to follow Him and to model His actions as we interact with other people and influence our culture. He will lead us to quiet water—places of safety where we can be refreshed.

**Do you live as if Jesus is your good Shepherd? In what practical ways do you see Him leading and caring for you?**

**What commitment are you willing to make to follow His leading?**

2.   *Sometimes life is difficult and can be compared to the vast wilderness areas of ancient Israel. Things are parched . . . confusing . . . and dangerous.* But God is our Shepherd—even in the wilderness. In fact, as we learn to trust Him and faithfully follow Him through the wilderness, the roots of our faith will grow strong.

**Think about a "wilderness" in which you have lived—or maybe are living today. What lessons did you learn through God's provision and guidance for you during that wilderness experience?**

**In what ways are you living in light of those lessons today?**

**In what ways do you need to remember what God did for you then?**

**What will you do to cultivate your ability to hear your Shepherd's voice in your wilderness?**

# closing prayer

I minute

Let's close in prayer now, thanking God for being our Shepherd.

*Dear God, thank You for being our Good Shepherd. It's amazing that You love us so much that You will lead us to green pastures daily in order to meet our needs. Just as Jesus followed the Father's leading when He walked on earth, we have the opportunity to follow Jesus and model His actions as we interact with other people. It's so easy to become sidetracked on the wrong paths. It's so easy to become discouraged in the wilderness. Draw us closer to You. Help us to listen for Your voice, and enable us to trust You more. In Jesus' name we pray, amen.*

**Action Points**

Take a moment to review the key points you explored today, then jot down an action step (or steps) that you will commit to this week as a result of what you have learned.

1.  *Jesus is our Good Shepherd; we are His sheep.* In much the same way that the shepherds of Israel's wilderness lead, protect, and nourish their flocks, Jesus will lead us to green pastures and provide us with what we need for today. He will walk before us, inviting us to follow Him and to model His actions as we interact with other people and influence our culture. He will lead us to quiet water—places of safety where we can be refreshed.

    **Do you live as if Jesus is your good Shepherd? In what practical ways do you see Him leading and caring for you?**

    **What commitment are you willing to make to follow His leading?**

2.  *Sometimes life is difficult and can be compared to the vast wilderness areas of ancient Israel. Things are parched ... confusing ... and dangerous.* But God is our Shepherd— even in the wilderness. In fact, as we learn to trust Him and faithfully follow Him through the wilderness, the roots of our faith will grow strong.

    **Think about a "wilderness" in which you have lived—or maybe are living today. What lessons did you learn**

through God's provision and guidance for you during that wilderness experience?

**In what ways are you living in light of those lessons today?**

**In what ways do you need to remember what God did for you then?**

**What will you do to cultivate your ability to hear your Shepherd's voice in your wilderness?**

PLANNING NOTES:

# god with us

## before you lead

### Synopsis

As far back as 3000 B.C., a large Canaanite city stood in the Negev where the small town of Arad sits today. In fact, the city existed when Abraham lived in the Negev. After the Canaanite city was destroyed, possibly by Joshua, the Israelites rebuilt and fortified it. During a period of 350 years, the Israelites rebuilt it at least six times. A unique series of historical events has preserved an archaeological treasure in Tel Arad that helps us better understand how the Hebrew people worshiped God.

When King Hezekiah came into power, many Israelites in the southern kingdom worshiped Canaanite gods. To prevent them from worshiping these gods and to pressure them to worship God in Jerusalem, King Hezekiah eliminated Baal worship and ordered the destruction of all shrines, altars, and high places (those dedicated to Yahweh as well as to Baal). So although the Israelites in Arad apparently worshiped and honored Yahweh—the true God—exclusively, they had to destroy their temple. Instead of tearing it down, however, they covered it with earth.

As you'll see in the video, the temple in Arad was modeled after the one in Jerusalem. It was smaller in size, but had the same courts and furnishings and an altar of the required dimensions. It had a Holy of Holies that represented God's dwelling place (the ark of the covenant, in which God actually lived, remained in the temple in Jerusalem), a court in which the priests worshiped, and a place in which the people worshiped. The recently uncovered temple in Arad is particularly significant because the Babylonian army completely destroyed Jerusalem in 586 B.C., leaving no remains of Solomon's temple.

After showing details about the temple in Arad, Ray Vander Laan explains the roots of the blood sacrifice that was central to the Israelites' worship of God. In order to seal His covenant with Abram (that God would make him the father of a great nation and give his descendants a land to live in), God asked Abram to gather five animals—a heifer, goat, ram, pigeon, and dove (Genesis 15:9). Abram was familiar with the ceremony used to make a covenant. The parties would gather the animals, cut each into two parts from nose to tail and place them on the ground so that their blood flowed together in one stream. Then the parties would walk in that blood, signifying what would happen if either party broke the covenant. So Abram gathered those animals, cut them in two, and allowed their blood to flow.

Later, "a thick and dreadful darkness" came over him as he slept (Genesis 15:12). He knew that if God participated in the covenant ceremony, he—a human—could never keep it perfectly and would face terrible consequences. But God, in effect, said, "If this covenant is ever broken, by you or by Me, My blood will cover the failure." After this time, animals sacrificed to God were a reminder of God's promise to forgive the people of Israel, a way in which they laid claim to God's promise of forgiveness and were cleansed from their guilt.

Within that ancient culture, each of the parties making a covenant (in this case God and the Israelites) also received a stone tablet. These tablets summarized the covenant. Each party then put the tablet they had been given into their most sacred shrine. In this case, God chose to keep His tablet containing the Ten Commandments in the same place as the Israelites' tablet—in the ark of the covenant.

Imagine how Moses felt when God gave him both tablets! God was saying, in effect, "My sacred and holy place is exactly the same as your sacred and holy place. What's holy to Me is holy to you. So keep both copies in the ark of the covenant. I love you so much that I'll come and live on the cover of the ark." So, God—the Creator—lived on the cover of a box that the Israelites initially carried on their shoulders. Later, God wanted the ark to be where anyone could find it and know that He was there. So He designated that it be placed in the Holy of Holies in the temple, which lit up with God's glory.

After the Babylonians destroyed the temple, instead of living on a box or in a building, God revealed His presence through His Son, Jesus, who lived on earth. Jesus put His arms around the hurting, sick, rich, poor, famous, and unimportant. He said, in effect, "I love you enough to live among you."

After Jesus died as our sacrificial Lamb, the power and presence of God came to live within His believers. Just as God chose to live on the ark of the covenant, Ray emphasizes, He has chosen to live within each believer. We are, as Paul writes, God's temple (1 Corinthians 6:19). So when people need to know that God is real and living among us, they need only to look at us. We bring His presence into our culture. What an opportunity! What a responsibility!

## Key Points of This Lesson

1. *God has chosen to reveal His presence to the world through His people.* During Old Testament times, God made a binding covenant with His people that was summarized on each of the two stone tablets He gave to Moses on Mount Sinai. To further emphasize His love and His desire to be with His people, God chose to live on the ark of the covenant in which the stone tablets were stored. The ark of the covenant, which was placed in the Holy of Holies in the temple, was literally God's dwelling place on earth.

   Thus the Ten Commandments, which were written on each of the two stone tablets, were far more than a checklist of God's requirements. They were a reminder of the covenant God had made with His people. The tablets said, in effect, "I am God. I love you enough to make a covenant with you through My own blood."

2. *When the temple in Jerusalem was destroyed, God's presence left the earth until He revealed it again through Jesus, His beloved Son.* In Jesus, God fulfilled the promise He had made to Abraham of giving His own life to seal the covenant He had made. Not only did the sovereign Creator live

among sinful human beings to demonstrate His presence, He offered His life to save those who had broken His covenant.

3. *Through Jesus' blood that was shed on the cross for our sins, God created a new covenant in which we—those who have accepted Jesus the Messiah as our Lord and Savior—have become His temple.* As we live in relationship with Him, we make His presence known to a spiritually needy world.

## Session Outline (55 minutes)

**I. Introduction** (4 minutes)

Welcome

What's to Come

Questions to Think About

**II. Show Video "God with Us"** (29 minutes)

**III. Group Discovery** (15 minutes)

Video Highlights

Small Group Bible Discovery

**IV. Faith Lesson** (6 minutes)

Time for Reflection

Action Points

**V. Closing Prayer** (1 minute)

## Materials

No additional materials are needed for this session. Simply view the video prior to leading the session so you are familiar with its main points.

# god with us

## introduction

**4** minutes

### Welcome

> Assemble the participants together. Welcome them to session six of *Faith Lessons on the Prophets and Kings of Israel.*

### What's to Come

In this session, Ray Vander Laan explores the ceremonies and structures the Israelites used to establish and develop their relationship with God—the same God we worship today. As we explore a newly discovered temple in Arad, we will come to understand more about the temple in Jerusalem and the covenant God established with His people through Abraham, Moses, David, and Solomon. We will see that God established principles of worship that anticipated Jesus' life and ministry more than a thousand years before He was born. We'll also be challenged—as temples of the Holy Spirit—to take God's presence into our culture, so that He can be seen by our world.

### Questions to Think About

> *Participant's Guide page 115.*

> Ask each question and solicit a few responses from group members.

1. What do the Ten Commandments signify to you? What was God's purpose for writing them?

   *Suggested Responses:* will vary but may include a set of rules Christians are to live by, rules given by God so we know what is right or wrong, etc. Encourage participants to consider what the Ten Commandments might signify more than a set of rules.

2. How can we know that God is real? What evidence of His presence can we see today?

   *Suggested Responses:* Allow participants to share how they know that God is real. See if they bring up how they see God demonstrated in the lives of His people.

Let's see what new possibilities we discover as we view the video.

**SESSION SIX**

# god with us

## questions to think about

1. What do the Ten Commandments signify to you? What was God's purpose for writing them?

2. How can we know that God is real? What evidence of His presence can we see today?

115

# video presentation

**29** minutes         | *Participant's Guide page 116.*

On page 116 of your Participant's Guide, you will find a space in which to take notes on key points as we watch this video.

### Leader's Video Observations

Arad and Its Temple

God's Covenant:

   With Abraham

   Moses and the Ten Commandments

   Jesus, the Covenant Sacrifice

   God's Dwelling Place Today

116       Faith Lessons on the Prophets and Kings of Israel

## video notes

**Arad and Its Temple**

**God's Covenant:**

With Abraham

Moses and the Ten Commandments

Jesus, the Covenant Sacrifice

**God's Dwelling Place Today**

# Group Discovery

If your group has seven or more members, use the **Video Highlights** with the entire group (4 minutes), then break into small groups of three to five to discuss the **Small Group Bible Discovery** (7 minutes). Then reassemble the group to discuss the key points discovered (4 minutes).

If your group has fewer than seven members, begin with the **Video Highlights** (4 minutes), then do one or more of the topics found in the **Small Group Bible Discovery** as a group (7 minutes). Finally, spend four minutes at the end discussing points that had an impact on participants.

### Video Highlights (4 minutes)

Here you'll ask one or more of the following questions that directly relate to the video the participants have just seen.

1. What do you observe about the location of Arad on the map on page 118? Why do you think the people built a temple there?

   *Suggested Responses:* Arad is a fairly remote city, with rugged mountains to the north and west, and the Negev wilderness to the south. Considering the number of times it was attacked and rebuilt, it must have been a strategic defense point for Israel. The people who lived there apparently were devoted to God and wanted to worship Him where they lived rather than in Jerusalem.

2. Why do you think God made specific covenants with Abraham and later with His people through Moses on Mount Sinai?

   *Suggested Responses:* God wanted to clearly communicate His love to them, as well as the standards by which He wanted them to live; He wanted them to have a record of the covenant so they could be reminded of His love for them; etc.

**Tel Arad**

## video highlights

1. What do you observe about the location of Arad on the map on page 118? Why do you think the people built a temple there?

2. Why do you think God made specific covenants with Abraham and later with His people through Moses on Mount Sinai?

**Tel Arad**

PLANNING NOTES:

✏ 3. How has learning about God's purpose for writing the Ten Commandments—to summarize His covenant and remind the Israelites of His love—
changed how you view them?

*Suggested Responses:* will vary. Encourage participants to rethink how they view
the Ten Commandments.

✏ 4. In light of the fact that the ark of the covenant in the temple was truly the
dwelling place of God, what difference should it make that Christian believers are now the temples of God?

*Suggested Responses:* It's important that people who seek to know God see Him
represented in us, and that we impact our culture in godly ways. Therefore, we
should seek to live holy lives, treat people as God would treat them, use our bodies according to the Bible's guidelines, and realize that God wants people to see
evidence of Him in everything we say and do.

**The Divided Kingdom**

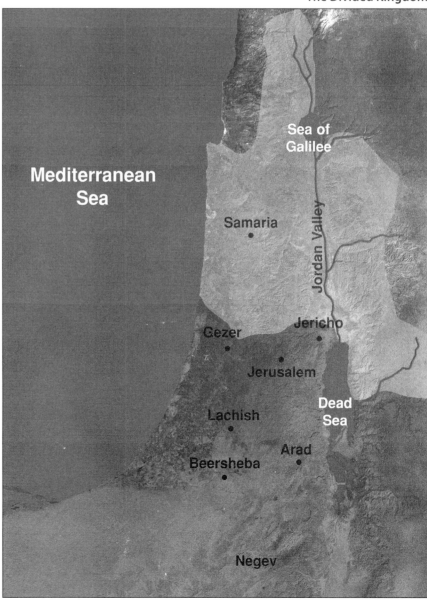

3. How has learning about God's purpose for writing the Ten Commandments—to summarize His covenant and remind the Israelites of His love—changed how you view them?

**The Divided Kingdom**

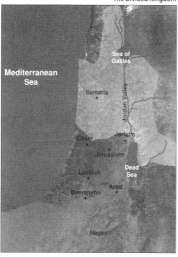

Mediterranean Sea

Sea of Galilee

Samaria

Jordan Valley

Gezer

Jericho

Jerusalem

Lachish

Dead Sea

Beersheba

Arad

Negev

4. In light of the fact that the ark of the covenant in the temple was truly the dwelling place of God, what difference should it make that Christian believers are now the temples of God?

### COMPELLING EVIDENCE

**Arad's God-fearing People**

Archaeologists at Arad, who believe the inhabitants who lived there nearly 3,000 years ago worshiped only *Yahweh*, have discovered the following items:

- Potsherds with writing on them (*ostraca*) inscribed with the names of priests mentioned in the Bible and Yahwistic names (that contain part of God's name).
- Bowls inscribed "Sons of Bezalel." (See Exodus 31:1–11.)
- An offering bowl inscribed "Sacred for the Priests."
- A temple similar in design to Solomon's temple in Jerusalem.

**The Temple at Arad**

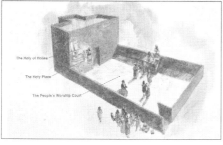

The Holy of Holies

The Holy Place

The People's Worship Court

## COMPELLING EVIDENCE

### Arad's God-fearing People

Archaeologists at Arad, who believe the inhabitants who lived there nearly 3,000 years ago worshiped only *Yahweh*, have discovered the following items:

- Potsherds with writing on them (*ostraca*) inscribed with the names of priests mentioned in the Bible and Yahwistic names (that contain part of God's name).
- Bowls inscribed "Sons of Bezalel." (See Exodus 31:1–11.)
- An offering bowl inscribed "Sacred for the Priests."
- A temple similar in design to Solomon's temple in Jerusalem.

**The Temple at Arad**

The Holy of Holies

The Holy Place

The People's Worship Court

## Small Group Bible Discovery (11 minutes)

> *Participant's Guide pages 120–133.*
>
> During this time, a group with fewer than seven participants will stay together. A group with seven or more participants will break into small groups and reassemble as a large group during the final four minutes. Assign each group one of the following topics. If you have more than five small groups, assign some topics to more than one group.

Let's break into groups of three to five—people sitting near you—and study some of the Bible passages and truths mentioned in the video.

Turn to pages 120–133 in your Participant's Guide. There you'll find a list of five topics. You'll have seven minutes to read and discuss the topic I'll assign to you. Choose one person in your group to be a spokesperson for your group when we discuss these topics later.

> Assign each group a topic.

I'll signal you when one minute is left.

4. In light of the fact that the ark of the covenant in the temple was truly the dwelling place of God, what difference should it make that Christian believers are now the temples of God?

### COMPELLING EVIDENCE

**Arad's God-fearing People**

Archaeologists at Arad, who believe the inhabitants who lived there nearly 3,000 years ago worshiped only *Yahweh*, have discovered the following items:

- Potsherds with writing on them (*ostraca*) inscribed with the names of priests mentioned in the Bible and Yahwistic names (that contain part of God's name).
- Bowls inscribed "Sons of Bezalel." (See Exodus 31:1–11.)
- An offering bowl inscribed "Sacred for the Priests."
- A temple similar in design to Solomon's temple in Jerusalem.

**The Temple at Arad**

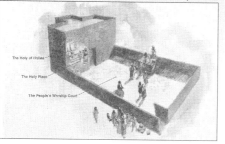

The Holy of Holies

The Holy Place

The People's Worship Court

## Topic A: Sacrifices in the Temple

1.  In ancient Israel, what did the animal sacrifices made on the temple altar signify? (See Leviticus 17:5–7, 11; Hebrews 9:22.)

    *Suggested Response:* The sacrifices, which involved the shedding of blood (the pouring out of the animal's life), symbolized the atonement made for the people's sins.

2.  According to God's command, what daily sacrifices were the Israelites to make? (See Numbers 28:1–8.)

    *Suggested Response:* A one-year-old, perfect lamb was to be sacrificed in the morning, and another year-old lamb was to be sacrificed at twilight. A grain offering and a drink offering were to be offered at the same times. These daily sacrifices were in addition to those specified for the Sabbath and other occasions.

**The Outer Court of the Temple at Arad**

3.  Describe the guidelines that God gave for the temple altar, which was to stand in the outer worship court. (See Exodus 20:25–26; 27:1.)

    *Suggested Response:* A stone altar was to be built without steps, using stones on which no tools had been used. A wooden altar was to be built of acacia wood and was to be three cubits (about 4 1/2 feet) high, five cubits (about 7 1/2 feet) long, and five cubits wide. (Note: The altar in Arad was made of uncut stones according to these specifications.)

4.  Describe the location and purpose of the bronze Sea. (See Exodus 30:17–21. Note: The bronze Sea of Solomon's temple is described in 2 Chronicles 4:2–5.)

    *Suggested Responses:* This metal basin stood in the outer worship court. The priests used the water in the basin for ceremonial cleansing before they approached the altar in order to minister to the Lord. (Note: The bronze Sea symbolized both the

120    Faith Lessons on the Prophets and Kings of Israel

## small Group Bible Discovery

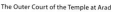

### Topic A: Sacrifices in the Temple

1. In ancient Israel, what did the animal sacrifices made on the temple altar signify? (See Leviticus 17:5–7, 11; Hebrews 9:22.)

2. According to God's command, what daily sacrifices were the Israelites to make? (See Numbers 28:1–8.)

**The Outer Court of the Temple at Arad**

---

Session Six: God with Us                    121

3. Describe the guidelines that God gave for the temple altar, which was to stand in the outer worship court. (See Exodus 20:25–26; 27:1.)

4. Describe the location and purpose of the bronze Sea. (See Exodus 30:17–21. Note: The bronze Sea of Solomon's temple is described in 2 Chronicles 4:2–5.)

5. Which imagery found in Acts 22:14–16 and 1 Corinthians 6:11 is similar in function to the bronze Sea?

removal of ceremonial uncleanness before the sacrifice was offered and the forgiveness resulting from the sacrifice itself.)

✏ 5.    Which imagery found in Acts 22:14–16 and 1 Corinthians 6:11 is similar in function to the bronze sea?

*Suggested Responses:* Both of these passages refer to the washing away of sins in the name of Jesus Christ. The Lord told Paul to be baptized, which is a type of ceremonial washing, and then to minister to God by being a witness to all men.

---

## DATA FILE

### The Temple Courts

The temple in Arad was built in a style probably influenced by Egyptian architecture and with materials similar to those used to build the average Israelite house. The temple in Jerusalem, on the other hand, was elaborately furnished and followed the Phoenician-Syrian temple design. Yet both temples contained the same courts and accomplished the same worship functions.

#### The Holy of Holies

(God's dwelling place) in Jerusalem contained the ark of the covenant, which held the tablets of the covenant (the Ten Commandments). In the temple in Arad, this area was reached by climbing two steps—symbolizing going up to God. Two standing stones were found in the temple in Arad. These stones may have represented the tablets of the Ten Commandments—God's covenant with Israel.

#### The Holy Place

(Priests' court) was a rectangular room between the worship court and the Holy of Holies that contained the table of showbread, golden lampstand, and the altar of incense. (The temple in Arad had two altars; the temple in Jerusalem had one.) The showbread was placed as an offering in the presence of God (Leviticus 24:5–9). This offering symbolized a thanksgiving gift to God as well as a request for His provision

(continued on page 210)

**The Temples at Arad and Jerusalem**

## DATA FILE

### The Temple Courts

The temple in Arad was built in a style probably influenced by Egyptian architecture and with materials similar to those used to build the average Israelite house. The temple in Jerusalem, on the other hand, was elaborately furnished and followed the Phoenician-Syrian temple design. Yet both temples contained the same courts and accomplished the same worship functions.

#### The Holy of Holies

(God's dwelling place) in Jerusalem contained the ark of the covenant, which held the tablets of the covenant (the Ten Commandments). In the temple in Arad, this area was reached by climbing two steps—symbolizing going up to God. Two standing stones were found in the temple in Arad. These stones may have represented the tablets of the Ten Commandments—God's covenant with Israel.

#### The Holy Place

(Priests' court) was a rectangular room between the worship court and the Holy of Holies that contained the table of showbread, golden lampstand, and the altar of incense. (The temple in Arad had two altars; the temple in Jerusalem had one.) The showbread was placed as an offering in the presence of God (Leviticus 24:5–9). This offering symbolized a thanksgiving gift to God as well as a request for His provision of food. The priests, on behalf of the people, ate the bread as a symbol of their relationship with God.

At Arad, the Holy Place was positioned so that its longest walls opened to the Worship Court on one side and the Holy of Holies on the other. (See the diagram of the two temples on page 123.) This style brought the people in the Worship Court closer to the priest in his room and to God in the Holy of Holies. So the room was called the "broad room."

In the temple in Jerusalem, the Holy Place's shortest walls bordered the Holy of Holies and the Worship Court, so the people were farther away from the priest and from God in the Holy of Holies. So the room was called the "long room."

#### The Worship Court

(The people's place) a large outer court in which the people stood to worship, contained the altar of sacrifice and the laver or basin (the bronze Sea).

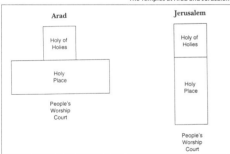

The Temples at Arad and Jerusalem

**Arad**
- Holy of Holies
- Holy Place
- People's Worship Court

**Jerusalem**
- Holy of Holies
- Holy Place
- People's Worship Court

Panarama of the Temple at Arad

(continued from page 208)

of food. The priests, on behalf of the people, ate the bread as a symbol of their relationship with God.

At Arad, the Holy Place was positioned so that its longest walls opened to the Worship Court on one side and the Holy of Holies on the other. (See the diagram of the two temples on page 123.) This style brought the people in the Worship Court closer to the priest in his room and to God in the Holy of Holies. So the room was called the "broad room."

In the temple in Jerusalem, the Holy Place's shortest walls bordered the Holy of Holies and the Worship Court, so the people were farther away from the priest and from God in the Holy of Holies. So the room was called the "long room."

### The Worship Court

(The people's place) a large outer court in which the people stood to worship, contained the altar of sacrifice and the laver or basin (the bronze Sea).

**Panarama of the Temple at Arad**

## Topic B: The Holy Places of the Temple

The altar and bronze Sea were positioned in the people's worship area of the temple. The temple also had a Holy Place for the priests, and the Holy of Holies, which was God's place. Note the purpose for the furnishings in these courts of the temple.

✏ 1.  Describe the table of showbread that God commanded Moses to make. (See Exodus 25:23–30.)

*Suggested Responses:* It was made of acacia wood, overlaid with pure gold, had a ring at each corner to hold the poles used to carry the table, had matching gold plates and dishes, and was two cubits (three feet) long, a cubit (one and a half feet) wide, and a cubit and a half (two and a quarter feet) high. On it were placed the bread offerings that symbolized a thanksgiving gift to God and a request for His continued provision.

### The Worship Court

(The people's place) a large outer court in which the people stood to worship, contained the altar of sacrifice and the laver or basin (the bronze Sea).

**The Temples at Arad and Jerusalem**

**Arad**

Holy of Holies

Holy Place

People's Worship Court

**Jerusalem**

Holy of Holies

Holy Place

People's Worship Court

**Panarama of the Temple at Arad**

---

### Topic B: The Holy Places of the Temple

The altar and bronze Sea were positioned in the people's worship area of the temple. The temple also had a Holy Place for the priests, and the Holy of Holies, which was God's place. Note the purpose for the furnishings in these courts of the temple.

1. Describe the table of showbread that God commanded Moses to make. (See Exodus 25:23–30.)

2. The golden lampstand stood in the Holy Place in front of the veil covering the Holy of Holies and represented God's presence. It was to be a reflection of His glory. How was the lampstand to be made? (See Exodus 25:31–32, 37–40; Numbers 8:3–4.)

3. During which hours of the day were the priests to keep the oil lamps on the lampstand burning? (See Exodus 27:20–21.)

4. How many of these lampstands did Solomon make for the first temple in Jerusalem? (See 2 Chronicles 4:7.)

2.  The golden lampstand stood in the Holy Place in front of the veil covering the Holy of Holies and represented God's presence. It was to be a reflection of His glory. How was the lampstand to be made? (See Exodus 25:31–32, 37–40; Numbers 8:3–4.)

    *Suggested Responses:* God gave the instructions for the lampstand to Moses on Mount Sinai. It had seven lamps (symbolizing completeness) and was hammered out of pure gold.

3.  During which hours of the day were the priests to keep the oil lamps on the lampstand burning? (See Exodus 27:20–21.)

    *Suggested Response:* From evening until morning.

4.  How many of these lampstands did Solomon make for the first temple in Jerusalem? (See 2 Chronicles 4:7.)

    *Suggested Response:* ten.

**The First Temple at Jerusalem**

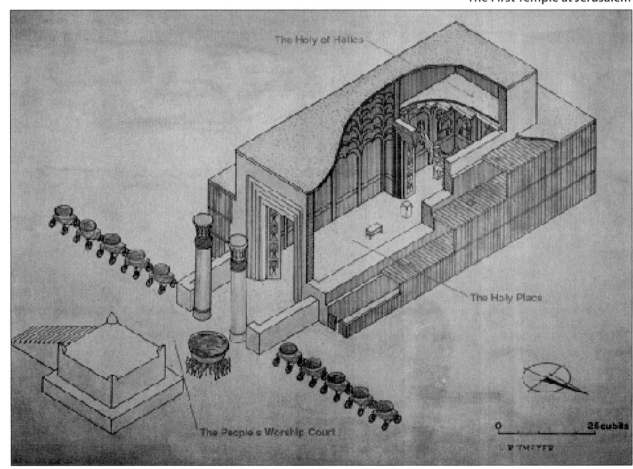

**Topic B: The Holy Places of the Temple**

The altar and bronze Sea were positioned in the people's worship area of the temple. The temple also had a Holy Place for the priests, and the Holy of Holies, which was God's place. Note the purpose for the furnishings in these courts of the temple.

1.  Describe the table of showbread that God commanded Moses to make. (See Exodus 25:23–30.)

2.  The golden lampstand stood in the Holy Place in front of the veil covering the Holy of Holies and represented God's presence. It was to be a reflection of His glory. How was the lampstand to be made? (See Exodus 25:31–32, 37–40; Numbers 8:3–4.)

3.  During which hours of the day were the priests to keep the oil lamps on the lampstand burning? (See Exodus 27:20–21.)

4.  How many of these lampstands did Solomon make for the first temple in Jerusalem? (See 2 Chronicles 4:7.)

**The First Temple at Jerusalem**

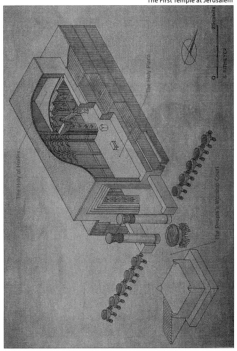

 5.   The altar of incense was located in front of the entrance to the Holy of Holies. The temple in Jerusalem had one altar of incense; the temple in Arad had two. What is the significance of the offering of incense? (See Exodus 30:7–8; Psalm 141:2; Revelation 5:8.)

*Suggested Response:* Incense was burned in the morning and at night when the priest tended the lamps. It represented the prayers of God's people. When the incense was placed on the altar, the smoke wafted up to heaven, just as the people's prayers rose up to God.

**The Holy Place of the Temple at Arad**

 6.   The ark of the covenant, which became the focus of God's presence among His people (Psalm 99:1), was kept in the Holy of Holies. Who was allowed into the Holy of Holies, and under what circumstances? (See Leviticus 16:2, 34. Note: Leviticus 16 specifies in detail the activities of the Day of Atonement.)

*Suggested Responses:* Only the high priest was allowed into this most sacred chamber, and only on the Day of Atonement. This is because God Himself appeared in the cloud over the cover of the ark of the covenant, and anyone who approached the Lord at any other time would die.

**DID YOU KNOW?**
Rather than choosing a unique design for His temple in Jerusalem, God chose a well-known, older design that followed the Phoenician-Syrian temple design. Huram-Abi, the man Hiram, king of Tyre, sent to Solomon to supervise construction of the temple, was well skilled in this design style. In fact, Scripture reveals that he was "trained to work in gold and silver, bronze and iron, stone and wood, and with purple and blue and crimson yarn and fine linen" (2 Chronicles 2:14). He also was an expert engraver!

5. The altar of incense was located in front of the entrance to the Holy of Holies. The temple in Jerusalem had one altar of incense; the temple in Arad had two. What is the significance of the offering of incense? (See Exodus 30:7–8; Psalm 141:2; Revelation 5:8.)

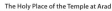

**The Holy Place of the Temple at Arad**

6. The ark of the covenant, which became the focus of God's presence among His people (Psalm 99:1), was kept in the Holy of Holies. Who was allowed into the Holy of Holies, and under what circumstances? (See Leviticus 16:2, 34. Note: Leviticus 16 specifies in detail the activities of the Day of Atonement.)

**DID YOU KNOW?**
Rather than choosing a unique design for His temple in Jerusalem, God chose a well-known, older design that followed the Phoenician-Syrian temple design. Huram-Abi, the man Hiram, king of Tyre, sent to Solomon to supervise construction of the temple, was well skilled in this design style. In fact, Scripture reveals that he was "trained to work in gold and silver, bronze and iron, stone and wood, and with purple and blue and crimson yarn and fine linen" (2 Chronicles 2:14). He also was an expert engraver!

**Topic C: God's Covenants with His People**
In the ancient Near East, there was a special covenant form in which a greater party (often a king) established a relationship with a lesser party (often a vassal). The greater party determined the responsibilities of each, and the lesser party accepted or rejected the relationship. God used this kind of covenant when dealing with His people.

1. The following verses each represent a covenant God made with people. For each, note (1) the person through whom God made the covenant; (2) why God, as the superior party, had the right to make the covenant; (3) what God promised within the relationship; and (4) any sign given as a symbol of the covenant.

| The Covenant | God's Right | God's Promise | The Sign |
|---|---|---|---|
| Genesis 9:8–17 | | | |
| Genesis 15:4–21; 17:1–11 | | | |

(continued on page 128)

### Topic C: God's Covenants with His People

In the ancient Near East, there was a special covenant form in which a greater party (often a king) established a relationship with a lesser party (often a vassal). The greater party determined the responsibilities of each, and the lesser party accepted or rejected the relationship. God used this kind of covenant when dealing with His people.

✏ 1.    The following verses each represent a covenant God made with people. For each, note (1) the person through whom God made the covenant; (2) why God, as the superior party, had the right to make the covenant; (3) what God promised within the relationship; and (4) any sign given as a symbol of the covenant.

| The Covenant | God's Right | God's Promise | The Sign |
|---|---|---|---|
| (with Noah) Genesis 9:8–17 | He is Creator of the universe who controls all of nature | to never again create a flood that would destroy all earthly life | a rainbow |
| (with Abraham) Genesis 15:4–21; 17:1–11 | He is God, who brought Abraham out of the land of Ur | to give him the land of Canaan, make him a father of nations, bless all nations through him | circumcision |
| (with the people of Israel, through Moses) Exodus 19:3–6; 24:3–8, 12; 31:18; 40:20–21 | He brought the Israelites up out of bondage in Egypt | they would be God's people, His holy nation, if they obeyed His laws | Moses offered a blood sacrifice and set up twelve stone pillars, God gave Moses the Ten Commandments to keep in the ark of the covenant |
| (with David) 2 Samuel 7:1–26 | He is the Lord Almighty who brought Israel out of Egypt and destroyed their enemies | to give rest to the people from their enemies, to establish David's throne forever, to make his name great | David's son (Solomon) would build God's temple |
| (with all believers) Hebrews 13:20; Luke 22:19–20; 1 Corinthians 5:7 | Jesus is God's perfect Son and our Good Shepherd | to be the Passover Lamb, who was sacrificed for our salvation | the bread and cup, symbolizing His broken body and shed blood |

**DID YOU KNOW?**

Rather than choosing a unique design for His temple in Jerusalem, God chose a well-known, older design that followed the Phoenician-Syrian temple design. Huram-Abi, the man Hiram, king of Tyre, sent to Solomon to supervise construction of the temple, was well skilled in this design style. In fact, Scripture reveals that he was "trained to work in gold and silver, bronze and iron, stone and wood, and with purple and blue and crimson yarn and fine linen" (2 Chronicles 2:14). He also was an expert engraver!

**Topic C: God's Covenants with His People**

In the ancient Near East, there was a special covenant form in which a greater party (often a king) established a relationship with a lesser party (often a vassal). The greater party determined the responsibilities of each, and the lesser party accepted or rejected the relationship. God used this kind of covenant when dealing with His people.

1.  The following verses each represent a covenant God made with people. For each, note (1) the person through whom God made the covenant; (2) why God, as the superior party, had the right to make the covenant; (3) what God promised within the relationship; and (4) any sign given as a symbol of the covenant.

| The Covenant | God's Right | God's Promise | The Sign |
|---|---|---|---|
| Genesis 9:8–17 | | | |
| Genesis 15:4–21; 17:1–11 | | | |

(continued on page 128)

(continued from page 127)

| The Covenant | God's Right | God's Promise | The Sign |
|---|---|---|---|
| Exodus 19:3–6; 24:3–8, 12; 31:18; 40:20–21 | | | |
| 2 Samuel 7:1–26 | | | |
| Hebrews 13:20; Luke 22:19–20; 1 Corinthians 5:7 | | | |

**DATA FILE**

**The Ark of the Covenant**
- Was uniquely designed by God before any other sacred object (Exodus 25:10–22).
- Was made of acacia wood commonly found in the Sinai Peninsula.
- Was three feet nine inches long, two feet three inches wide, and two feet three inches high.
- Had gold plating and a golden rim around the top.
- Stood on four legs.
- Contained two gold rings on each side so the Levites—the priestly tribe—could insert poles into it and carry it.
- Had a cover (the mercy seat or atonement seat) made of pure gold.
- Two cherubim—probably sphinxes with wings outstretched—were positioned on top of the lid. They expressed the people's longing to feel safe in God's sheltering arms. The ark assured them that the holy God of Abraham was sovereign over all things and was a protecting, forgiving presence in their lives. (See 1 Chronicles 28:2 and Psalm 99:1.)

PLANNING NOTES:

**DATA FILE**

**The Ark of the Covenant**
- Was uniquely designed by God before any other sacred object (Exodus 25:10–22).
- Was made of acacia wood commonly found in the Sinai Peninsula.
- Was three feet nine inches long, two feet three inches wide, and two feet three inches high.
- Had gold plating and a golden rim around the top.
- Stood on four legs.
- Contained two gold rings on each side so the Levites—the priestly tribe—could insert poles into it and carry it.
- Had a cover (the mercy seat or atonement seat) made of pure gold.
- Two cherubim—probably sphinxes with wings outstretched—were positioned on top of the lid. They expressed the people's longing to feel safe in God's sheltering arms. The ark assured them that the holy God of Abraham was sovereign over all things and was a protecting, forgiving presence in their lives. (See 1 Chronicles 28:2 and Psalm 99:1.)

**SURPRISE!**

Traditionally, Christians have believed there were two tablets of the Law: one tablet (commandments 1–4) describing what our relationship with God should be; the other (commandments 5–10) describing what our relationship with other members of the covenant should be.

Although it is correct to divide the commandments into these two categories, nothing in Scripture supports the idea of two partial tablets. Everything we know about Israelite culture points to all ten commandments being written on each tablet. God gave both copies to Moses because God's sacred place and Moses' sacred place were the same: the ark of the covenant.

## Topic D: Jesus, the Sacrifice for Our Sins

1. Hundreds of years before Jesus, what did the prophet Isaiah say that Jesus would do for us? (See Isaiah 53:4–6, 11–12.)

   *Suggested Responses:* Jesus would be pierced for our sins, would carry our sorrows, and by His wounds we would be healed. God would place all our sins upon Jesus. Jesus would pour out His life to make intercession for all sinners.

2. What terminology did John the Baptist use to describe Jesus? (See John 1:29.)

   *Suggested Response:* John used the term "Lamb of God."

3. What is Jesus called in 1 Corinthians 5:7?

   *Suggested Response:* Jesus is called our Passover Lamb, who was sacrificed for us.

(continued from page 127)

| The Covenant | God's Right | God's Promise | The Sign |
|---|---|---|---|
| Exodus 19:3–6; 24:3–8, 12; 31:18; 40:20–21 | | | |
| 2 Samuel 7:1–26 | | | |
| Hebrews 13:20; Luke 22:19–20; 1 Corinthians 5:7 | | | |

### DATA FILE

**The Ark of the Covenant**
- Was uniquely designed by God before any other sacred object (Exodus 25:10–22).
- Was made of acacia wood commonly found in the Sinai Peninsula.
- Was three feet nine inches long, two feet three inches wide, and two feet three inches high.
- Had gold plating and a golden rim around the top.
- Stood on four legs.
- Contained two gold rings on each side so the Levites—the priestly tribe—could insert poles into it and carry it.
- Had a cover (the mercy seat or atonement seat) made of pure gold.
- Two cherubim—probably sphinxes with wings outstretched—were positioned on top of the lid. They expressed the people's longing to feel safe in God's sheltering arms. The ark assured them that the holy God of Abraham was sovereign over all things and was a protecting, forgiving presence in their lives. (See 1 Chronicles 28:2 and Psalm 99:1.)

### SURPRISE!

Traditionally, Christians have believed there were two tablets of the Law: one tablet (commandments 1–4) describing what our relationship with God should be; the other (commandments 5–10) describing what our relationship with other members of the covenant should be.

Although it is correct to divide the commandments into these two categories, nothing in Scripture supports the idea of two partial tablets. Everything we know about Israelite culture points to all ten commandments being written on each tablet. God gave both copies to Moses because God's sacred place and Moses' sacred place were the same: the ark of the covenant.

### Topic D: Jesus, the Sacrifice for Our Sins

1. Hundreds of years before Jesus, what did the prophet Isaiah say that Jesus would do for us? (See Isaiah 53:4–6, 11–12.)

2. What terminology did John the Baptist use to describe Jesus? (See John 1:29.)

3. What is Jesus called in 1 Corinthians 5:7?

✎ 4.   In light of the terminology used in the two Scripture references above, what is the significance of the specific time at which Jesus died on the cross? (See Matthew 27:46–50.)

*Suggested Response:* Jesus died about 3:00 in the afternoon, the same time as the Passover lamb was being sacrificed at the temple to atone for the people's sins.

✎ 5.   What does Hebrews 9:11–14 reveal about Jesus the Messiah's impact on the Israelites' central act of worship—blood sacrifices?

*Suggested Response:* All the sacrifices pointed to, and were fulfilled by, Jesus Christ. He—our High Priest—entered God's presence through His own blood that He shed for us. Through His blood, we can be cleansed from sin and serve the living God.

✎ 6.   After both temples were destroyed, Jewish followers of Yahweh pointed to passages like Micah 6:6–8 to indicate that obedience to God is the "new" sacrifice. How is that passage similar to Romans 12:1?

*Suggested Response:* The Micah passage reveals that God wants us to act justly, love mercy, and walk humbly with Him. Romans 12:1 tells us to offer our bodies as living sacrifices, holy and pleasing to God.

## DATA FILE

**The Preparation for Jesus' Coming—Fulfillment of a Promise**

God's covenant with Abraham demonstrated the *promise of God.* He declared His commitment to the Israelites by walking the blood path to make a covenant with Abraham and his descendants.

Through the tabernacle, ark of the covenant, and temple, God's people experienced the *presence of God.* God began restoring His presence among His people.

The tablets of the Ten Commandments sealed the *relationship between the people and their God.*

Although these commitments spectacularly demonstrated God's love, they anticipated an even greater act of love: the birth of God's own Son. The person of Jesus would fulfill everything that had come before. God would walk with His people, as He had walked with Adam and Eve. The blood of Jesus the Lamb would atone for the sins of those who believed in Him. In Jesus, God would reaffirm His dedication to the covenant relationship He made with His servant Abraham.

In Jesus, God fulfilled the promise He made to the Hebrews of giving His own life to seal the covenant He had made with them. For this reason, Jesus could say, "Do not think that I have come to abolish the Law or the Prophets; I have not come to abolish them but to fulfill them" (Matthew 5:17).

God's choice of the covenant to describe His relationship with His people highlights the degree of His love for us. Not only did the great sovereign Creator of heaven and earth descend to be in relationship with sinful human beings, He offered His life to provide escape for the very people who would violate His covenant! People of the ancient Near East cultures understood what a covenant was and recognized the indescribable gift of relationship God had given to those who believed in Him. It should be no less for us.

4. In light of the terminology used in the two Scripture references above, what is the significance of the specific time at which Jesus died on the cross? (See Matthew 27:46–50.)

5. What does Hebrews 9:11–14 reveal about Jesus the Messiah's impact on the Israelites' central act of worship—blood sacrifices?

6. After both temples were destroyed, Jewish followers of Yahweh pointed to passages like Micah 6:6–8 to indicate that obedience to God is the "new" sacrifice. How is that passage similar to Romans 12:1?

## DATA FILE

**The Preparation for Jesus' Coming—Fulfillment of a Promise**

God's covenant with Abraham demonstrated the *promise of God*. He declared His commitment to the Israelites by walking the blood path to make a covenant with Abraham and his descendants.

Through the tabernacle, ark of the covenant, and temple, God's people experienced the *presence of God*. God began restoring His presence among His people.

The tablets of the Ten Commandments sealed the *relationship between the people and their God*.

Although these commitments spectacularly demonstrated God's love, they anticipated an even greater act of love: the birth of God's own Son. The person of Jesus would fulfill everything that had come before. God would walk with His people, as He had walked with Adam and Eve. The blood of Jesus the Lamb would atone for the sins of those who believed in Him. In Jesus, God would reaffirm His dedication to the covenant relationship He made with His servant Abraham.

In Jesus, God fulfilled the promise He made to the Hebrews of giving His own life to seal the covenant He had made with them. For this reason, Jesus could say, "Do not think that I have come to abolish the Law or the Prophets; I have not come to abolish them but to fulfill them" (Matthew 5:17).

God's choice of the covenant to describe His relationship with His people highlights the degree of His love for us. Not only did the great sovereign Creator of heaven and earth descend to be in relationship with sinful human beings, He offered His life to provide escape for the very people who would violate His covenant! People of the ancient Near East cultures understood what a covenant was and recognized the indescribable gift of relationship God had given to those who believed in Him. It should be no less for us.

PLANNING NOTES:

## Topic E: God's Presence in the World

1. How near to His creation was God when He first created the world? What changed? (See Genesis 3:8, 23–24.)

   *Suggested Responses:* He was so close to His creation that Adam and Eve heard Him walking in the garden during the cool part of the day! Because of their sin against Him, God drove them away from His holy presence and wouldn't allow them back into the Garden of Eden.

2. What does Genesis 11:1–5 reveal about God's concern for His world?

   *Suggested Response:* God came down to see the city and the Tower of Babel that the world's people were building. Clearly God is aware of what is happening in the world.

3. What was the main purpose of the temple in Jerusalem? (See 2 Chronicles 5:7; 7:1–3.)

   *Suggested Response:* It was the place in which God resided, on the ark of the covenant within the Holy of Holies. The temple was built to reveal the glory of the Lord to the Israelites and all the world.

4. What happened to God's presence because of Israel's unbelief? (See Ezekiel 10:18–19.)

   *Suggested Response:* God's presence left the temple.

5. How did God restore His presence among His people? (See John 1:1, 14.)

   *Suggested Response:* Jesus the Messiah—the Word—became flesh and came to live on earth to reveal the glory of the Father.

6. In what way does God choose to reveal His presence today? (See 1 Corinthians 3:16–17.)

   *Suggested Response:* Today God's Spirit lives in every believer. Each believer is a temple of the Holy Spirit.

> After six minutes, let participants know that they have one minute remaining. Then reassemble the entire group. After everyone is back together, begin asking one person from each small group to briefly share a key idea with the larger group. In some cases, you may not have time for every group to share their discoveries.

As time allows, let's briefly share the key ideas that your group discussed.

## Topic E: God's Presence in the World

1. How near to His creation was God when He first created the world? What changed? (See Genesis 3:8, 23–24.)

2. What does Genesis 11:1–5 reveal about God's concern for His world?

3. What was the main purpose of the temple in Jerusalem? (See 2 Chronicles 5:7; 7:1–3.)

4. What happened to God's presence because of Israel's unbelief? (See Ezekiel 10:18–19.)

5. How did God restore His presence among His people? (See John 1:1, 14.)

6. In what way does God choose to reveal His presence today? (See 1 Corinthians 3:16–17.)

### PROVOCATIVE EVIDENCE

**Where God Dwells**

The Scriptures reveal some remarkable parallels between God's home in heaven and His former home on earth in the temple in Jerusalem:

| Heaven | Temple |
|---|---|
| God's dwelling place (2 Chronicles 6:21) | God's dwelling place (2 Chronicles 6:1–2) |
| God surrounded by cherubim (Revelation 4:6b–8; Ezekiel 1:6,10) | God surrounded by figures of cherubim (2 Chronicles 3:10–13) |
| God surrounded by His heavenly hosts (Revelation 5:11) | God surrounded by His earthly hosts (Numbers 2) |
| God is seated on a throne (Revelation 4:2–5) | The ark is God's throne (Psalm 99:1) |
| Altar representing the blood of the saints (Revelation 6:9) | Blood is sprinkled on the altar (Leviticus 1:10–11) |
| Prayers of the saints viewed as incense (Revelation 5:8) | Priest met with God at the altar of incense (Exodus 30:1,6) |
| Sea of crystal (Revelation 4:6) | Sea of bronze (1 Kings 7:23) |

## PROVOCATIVE EVIDENCE

### Where God Dwells

The Scriptures reveal some remarkable parallels between God's home in heaven and His former home on earth in the temple in Jerusalem:

| Heaven | Temple |
|---|---|
| God's dwelling place (2 Chronicles 6:21) | God's dwelling place (2 Chronicles 6:1–2) |
| God surrounded by cherubim (Revelation 4:6b–8; Ezekiel 1:6,10) | God surrounded by figures of cherubim (2 Chronicles 3:10–13) |
| God surrounded by His heavenly hosts (Revelation 5:11) | God surrounded by His earthly hosts (Numbers 2) |
| God is seated on a throne (Revelation 4:2–5) | The ark is God's throne (Psalm 99:1) |
| Altar representing the blood of the saints (Revelation 6:9) | Blood is sprinkled on the altar (Leviticus 1:10–11) |
| Prayers of the saints viewed as incense (Revelation 5:8) | Priest met with God at the altar of incense (Exodus 30:1,6) |
| Sea of crystal (Revelation 4:6) | Sea of bronze (1 Kings 7:23) |

# faith Lesson

**6** minutes

### Time for Reflection (4 minutes)

On page 134–135 of the Participant's Guide, you'll find a passage of Scripture. Let's each read this passage silently and take the next few minutes to consider some of the questions that follow the Scripture passage.

Please do not talk during this time. It's a time when we can reflect on how God would have us view our covenant with Him.

*The Scripture passage and questions are reproduced in their entirety in the Participant's Guide on pages 134–135.*

And God spoke all these words: "I am the LORD your God, who brought you out of Egypt, out of the land of slavery. You shall have no other gods before me. You shall not make for yourself an idol in the form of anything in heaven above or on the earth beneath or in the waters below. You shall not bow down to them or worship them; for I, the LORD your God, am a jealous God, punishing the children for the sin of the fathers to the third and fourth generation of those who hate me, but showing love to a thousand [generations] of those who love me and keep my commandments. You shall not

6. In what way does God choose to reveal His presence today? (See 1 Corinthians 3:16–17.)

### PROVOCATIVE EVIDENCE

**Where God Dwells**

The Scriptures reveal some remarkable parallels between God's home in heaven and His former home on earth in the temple in Jerusalem:

| Heaven | Temple |
| --- | --- |
| God's dwelling place (2 Chronicles 6:21) | God's dwelling place (2 Chronicles 6:1–2) |
| God surrounded by cherubim (Revelation 4:6b–8; Ezekiel 1:6,10) | God surrounded by figures of cherubim (2 Chronicles 3:10–13) |
| God surrounded by His heavenly hosts (Revelation 5:11) | God surrounded by His earthly hosts (Numbers 2) |
| God is seated on a throne (Revelation 4:2–5) | The ark is God's throne (Psalm 99:1) |
| Altar representing the blood of the saints (Revelation 6:9) | Blood is sprinkled on the altar (Leviticus 1:10–11) |
| Prayers of the saints viewed as incense (Revelation 5:8) | Priest met with God at the altar of incense (Exodus 30:1,6) |
| Sea of crystal (Revelation 4:6) | Sea of bronze (1 Kings 7:23) |

## faith Lesson

### Time for Reflection

Read the following passage of Scripture and take the next few minutes to consider how God would have you view your covenant with Him.

And God spoke all these words: "I am the LORD your God, who brought you out of Egypt, out of the land of slavery. You shall have no other gods before me. You shall not make for yourself an idol in the form of anything in heaven above or on the earth beneath or in the waters below. You shall not bow down to them or worship them; for I, the LORD your God, am a jealous God, punishing the children for the sin of the fathers to the third and fourth generation of those who hate me, but showing love to a thousand [generations] of those who love me and keep my commandments. You shall not misuse the name of the LORD your God, for the LORD will not hold anyone guiltless who misuses his name. Remember the Sabbath day by keeping it holy. Six days you shall labor and do all your work, but the seventh day is a Sabbath to the LORD your God. On it you shall not do any work, neither you, nor your son or daughter, nor your manservant or maidservant, nor your animals, nor the alien within your gates. For in six days the LORD made the heavens and the earth, the sea, and all that is in them, but he rested on the seventh day. Therefore the LORD blessed the Sabbath day and made it holy. "Honor your father and your mother, so that you may live long in the land the LORD your God is giving you. You shall not murder. You shall not commit adultery. You shall not steal. You shall not give false testimony against your neighbor. You shall not covet your neighbor's house. You shall not covet your neighbor's wife, or his manservant or maidservant, his ox or donkey, or anything that belongs to your neighbor." When the people saw the thunder and lightning and heard the trumpet and saw the mountain in smoke, they trembled with fear. They stayed at a distance and said to Moses, "Speak to us

misuse the name of the LORD your God, for the LORD will not hold anyone guiltless who misuses his name. Remember the Sabbath day by keeping it holy. Six days you shall labor and do all your work, but the seventh day is a Sabbath to the LORD your God. On it you shall not do any work, neither you, nor your son or daughter, nor your manservant or maidservant, nor your animals, nor the alien within your gates. For in six days the LORD made the heavens and the earth, the sea, and all that is in them, but he rested on the seventh day. Therefore the LORD blessed the Sabbath day and made it holy. Honor your father and your mother, so that you may live long in the land the LORD your God is giving you. You shall not murder. You shall not commit adultery. You shall not steal. You shall not give false testimony against your neighbor. You shall not covet your neighbor's house. You shall not covet your neighbor's wife, or his manservant or maidservant, his ox or donkey, or anything that belongs to your neighbor." When the people saw the thunder and lightning and heard the trumpet and saw the mountain in smoke, they trembled with fear. They stayed at a distance and said to Moses, "Speak to us yourself and we will listen. But do not have God speak to us or we will die." Moses said to the people, "Do not be afraid. God has come to test you, so that the fear of God will be with you to keep you from sinning."

EXODUS 20:1–20

1. How does your view of the Ten Commandments change when you read it as a statement of God's love and commitment to you rather than just a list of dos and don'ts?

2. What does it mean to you that God was willing to shed His own blood and die in order to pay for your violation of His covenant?

3. You are to your world what the ark of the covenant and the temple were to Israel—God's dwelling place. How, then, should you live so that the world may know that He is God?

4. The people of Arad left a God-fearing legacy behind. Looking back on your life, how do you think people will remember you? Which of your possessions testify to your faith in God? Which don't?

## Action Points (2 minutes)

*The following points are reproduced on page 136–137 of the Participant's Guide:*

Now it's time to wrap up our session.

**Give participants a moment to transition from their thoughtfulness to giving you their full attention.**

I'd like to take a moment to summarize the key points we explored. After I have reviewed these points, I will give you a moment to jot down an action step (or steps) that you will commit to this week as a result of what you have learned today.

yourself and we will listen. But do not have God speak to us or we will die." Moses said to the people, "Do not be afraid. God has come to test you, so that the fear of God will be with you to keep you from sinning."

EXODUS 20:1–20

1. How does your view of the Ten Commandments change when you read it as a statement of God's love and commitment to you rather than just a list of dos and don'ts?

2. What does it mean to you that God was willing to shed His own blood and die in order to pay for your violation of His covenant?

3. You are to your world what the ark of the covenant and the temple were to Israel—God's dwelling place. How, then, should you live so that the world may know that He is God?

4. The people of Arad left a God-fearing legacy behind. Looking back on your life, how do you think people will remember you? Which of your possessions testify to your faith in God? Which don't?

**Action Points**

Review the key points you explored today, then jot down an action step (or steps) that you will commit to this week as a result of what you have learned.

1. *God has chosen to reveal His presence to the world through His people.* During Old Testament times, God made a binding covenant with His people that was summarized on each of the two stone tablets He gave to Moses on Mount Sinai. To further emphasize His love and His desire to be with His people, God chose to live on the ark of the covenant in which the stone tablets were stored. The ark of the covenant, which was placed in the Holy of Holies in the temple, was literally God's dwelling place on earth.

   Thus the Ten Commandments, which were written on each of the two stone tablets, were far more than a checklist of God's requirements. They were a reminder of the covenant God had made with His people. The tablets said, in effect, "I am God. I love you enough to make a covenant with you through My own blood."

   **What in your life reminds you of God's deep love for you and His ongoing commitment to you?**

2. *When the temple in Jerusalem was destroyed, God's presence left the earth until He revealed it again through Jesus, His beloved Son.* In Jesus, God fulfilled the promise He had made to Abraham of giving His own life to seal the covenant He had made. Not only did the sovereign Creator live among sinful human beings to demonstrate His presence, He offered His life to save those who had broken His covenant.

> Read the following points and pause afterward so that participants can consider and write out their commitment.

1. *God has chosen to reveal His presence to the world through His people.* During Old Testament times, God made a binding covenant with His people that was summarized on each of the two stone tablets He gave to Moses on Mount Sinai. To further emphasize His love and His desire to be with His people, God chose to live on the ark of the covenant in which the stone tablets were stored. The ark of the covenant, which was placed in the Holy of Holies in the temple, was literally God's dwelling place on earth.

   Thus the Ten Commandments, which were written on each of the two stone tablets, were far more than a checklist of God's requirements. They were a reminder of the covenant God had made with His people. The tablets said, in effect, "I am God. I love you enough to make a covenant with you through My own blood."

   **What in your life reminds you of God's deep love for you and His ongoing commitment to you?**

2. *When the temple in Jerusalem was destroyed, God's presence left the earth until He revealed it again through Jesus, His beloved Son.* In Jesus, God fulfilled the promise He had made to Abraham of giving His own life to seal the covenant He had made. Not only did the sovereign Creator live among sinful human beings to demonstrate His presence, He offered His life to save those who had broken His covenant.

3. *Through Jesus' blood that was shed on the cross for our sins, God created a new covenant in which we—those who have accepted Jesus the Messiah as our Lord and Savior—have become His temple.* As we live in relationship with Him, we make His presence known to a spiritually needy world.

   **What do people see when they see you? In what way(s) are you revealing God's presence and power to a watching world?**

   **What will you do this week to more effectively present the reality of God's presence to the world around you? Be specific!**

**Action Points**

Review the key points you explored today, then jot down an action step (or steps) that you will commit to this week as a result of what you have learned.

1. *God has chosen to reveal His presence to the world through His people.* During Old Testament times, God made a binding covenant with His people that was summarized on each of the two stone tablets He gave to Moses on Mount Sinai. To further emphasize His love and His desire to be with His people, God chose to live on the ark of the covenant in which the stone tablets were stored. The ark of the covenant, which was placed in the Holy of Holies in the temple, was literally God's dwelling place on earth.

   Thus the Ten Commandments, which were written on each of the two stone tablets, were far more than a checklist of God's requirements. They were a reminder of the covenant God had made with His people. The tablets said, in effect, "I am God. I love you enough to make a covenant with you through My own blood."

   **What in your life reminds you of God's deep love for you and His ongoing commitment to you?**

2. *When the temple in Jerusalem was destroyed, God's presence left the earth until He revealed it again through Jesus, His beloved Son.* In Jesus, God fulfilled the promise He had made to Abraham of giving His own life to seal the covenant He had made. Not only did the sovereign Creator live among sinful human beings to demonstrate His presence, He offered His life to save those who had broken His covenant.

3. *Through Jesus' blood that was shed on the cross for our sins, God created a new covenant in which we—those who have accepted Jesus the Messiah as our Lord and Savior—have become His temple.* As we live in relationship with Him, we make His presence known to a spiritually needy world.

   **What do people see when they see you? In what way(s) are you revealing God's presence and power to a watching world?**

   **What will you do this week to more effectively present the reality of God's presence to the world around you? Be specific!**

**DATA FILE**

**Covenant Forms**

Ancient Near Eastern covenants, especially those between unequal parties, formed complex relationships. Many factors had to be considered: the right of the greater party to make the covenant, obligations of each party, penalties and benefits of the relationship, and the relationship's history. So, covenantal documents were usually quite long. God's covenant with Israel through Moses, for example, is recorded in the Torah—the first five books of the Bible. God's covenant with believers in Jesus is described in all sixty-six books of the Bible.

Covenants were carefully recorded and preserved. They were to be read regularly and always obeyed. Moses, for example, wrote down the words of God's covenant with His people in the Torah and commanded that it be read every seven years (Deuteronomy 31:9–13, 24–26). The

(continued on page 138)

# closing prayer

1 minute In this session, we've been challenged to remember that we are God's temple and as such are called to represent Him to a watching world. Let's close in prayer.

*Dear God, many years ago the Israelites worshiped You and lived in covenant with You. Today, because Jesus shed His blood for us on the cross, every person has the opportunity to have a personal relationship with You and to be Your temple. Please empower us to live out that high calling, to be Your representatives to the people in our neighborhoods, at work, in our families. Thank You that You love us so much that You want to be in relationship with us. In Your name we pray, Jesus. Amen.*

## DATA FILE

### Covenant Forms

Ancient Near Eastern covenants, especially those between unequal parties, formed complex relationships. Many factors had to be considered: the right of the greater party to make the covenant, obligations of each party, penalties and benefits of the relationship, and the relationship's history. So covenantal documents were usually quite long. God's covenant with Israel through Moses, for example, is recorded in the Torah—the first five books of the Bible. God's covenant with believers in Jesus is described in all sixty-six books of the Bible.

Covenants were carefully recorded and preserved. They were to be read regularly and always obeyed. Moses, for example, wrote down the words of God's covenant with His people in the Torah and commanded that it be read every seven years (Deuteronomy 31:9–13, 24–26). The summary document—the Ten Commandments—was stored in the most sacred place: the ark of the covenant, God's earthly throne.

In order to make sense of covenants, people followed a certain pattern that governed the materials contained in a covenant, including its content and form. A summary document representing the entirety of the relationship and following the accepted form of a covenant document was also provided.

Keeping in mind that God cut covenants as the superior party so that He alone determined their content, let's briefly review the components of the covenant God made with the Israelites.

### The Preamble

It identified the two parties of the covenant. In the Torah, God established the identities of the parties in the creation story. He was the Creator, and Israel was His creation. In the covenant summary (the Ten Commandments), He said simply, "I am the LORD your God" (Exodus 20:2).

(continued on page 232)

3.  *Through Jesus' blood that was shed on the cross for our sins,
    God created a new covenant in which we—those who have
    accepted Jesus the Messiah as our Lord and Savior—have
    become His temple.* As we live in relationship with Him,
    we make His presence known to a spiritually needy world.

    What do people see when they see you? In what way(s)
    are you revealing God's presence and power to a watch-
    ing world?

    What will you do this week to more effectively present
    the reality of God's presence to the world around you? Be
    specific!

**DATA FILE**

**Covenant Forms**
Ancient Near Eastern covenants, especially those between unequal parties, formed complex relationships. Many factors had to be considered:
the right of the greater party to make the covenant, obligations of each
party, penalties and benefits of the relationship, and the relationship's
history. So, covenantal documents were usually quite long. God's
covenant with Israel through Moses, for example, is recorded in the
Torah—the first five books of the Bible. God's covenant with believers in
Jesus is described in all sixty-six books of the Bible.
  Covenants were carefully recorded and preserved. They were to be
read regularly and always obeyed. Moses, for example, wrote down the
words of God's covenant with His people in the Torah and commanded
that it be read every seven years (Deuteronomy 31:9–13, 24–26). The

(continued on page 138)

(continued from page 137)
summary document—the Ten Commandments—was stored in the
most sacred place: the ark of the covenant, God's earthly throne.
  In order to make sense of covenants, people followed a certain pattern that governed the materials contained in a covenant, including its
content and form. A summary document representing the entirety of the
relationship and following the accepted form of a covenant document
was also provided.
  Keeping in mind that God cut covenants as the superior party so that
He alone determined their content, let's briefly review the components
of the covenant God made with the Israelites.

*The Preamble*
It identified the two parties of the covenant. In the Torah, God established the identities of the parties in the creation story. He was the Creator, and Israel was His creation. In the covenant summary (the Ten
Commandments), He said simply, "I am the LORD your God" (Exodus 20:2).

*The Historical Prologue*
The history leading to the cutting of the covenant was recited to prove
the right of the superior party to make it. In the Ten Commandments, for
example, the summary is simply, ". . . who brought you out of Egypt, out
of the land of slavery" (Exodus 20:2).

*Requirements (Commandments)*
The Torah contains 613 of the requirements God placed on the people
with whom He was in relationship. He placed even more obligations on
Himself. In summarizing the commandments, these requirements were
simplified to ten (Exodus 20:3–17). Some scholars have noted that Jesus
reduced His summary to just two obligations (Matthew 22:37–40).

*Blessings and Curses*
Keeping a covenant brought specific rewards, and breaking it
brought specific penalties. The Torah, for example, contains many blessings and curses.

(continued from page 230)

### The Historical Prologue

The history leading to the cutting of the covenant was recited to prove the right of the superior party to make it. In the Ten Commandments, for example, the summary is simply, "…who brought you out of Egypt, out of the land of slavery" (Exodus 20:2).

### Requirements (Commandments)

The Torah contains 613 of the requirements God placed on the people with whom He was in relationship. He placed even more obligations on Himself. In summarizing the commandments, these requirements were simplified to ten (Exodus 20:3–17). Some scholars have noted that Jesus reduced His summary to just two obligations (Matthew 22:37–40).

### Blessings and Curses

Keeping a covenant brought specific rewards, and breaking it brought specific penalties. The Torah, for example, contains many blessings and curses.

### The Summary Document

The short summary document, which could be easily read and stored, summarized the entire covenant and so represented the total relationship between the parties. Normally in Near Eastern culture, two summary documents were made; each party kept one in a sacred place. So, it seems clear that each tablet of the Ten Commandments contained all of the commandments. One copy was God's, and the other belonged to the people of Israel. Part of the purpose of the ark of the covenant was to hold the Ten Commandments, the summary of God's covenant with His people.

(continued from page 137)

summary document—the Ten Commandments—was stored in the most sacred place: the ark of the covenant, God's earthly throne.

In order to make sense of covenants, people followed a certain pattern that governed the materials contained in a covenant, including its content and form. A summary document representing the entirety of the relationship and following the accepted form of a covenant document was also provided.

Keeping in mind that God cut covenants as the superior party so that He alone determined their content, let's briefly review the components of the covenant God made with the Israelites.

### The Preamble

It identified the two parties of the covenant. In the Torah, God established the identities of the parties in the creation story. He was the Creator, and Israel was His creation. In the covenant summary (the Ten Commandments), He said simply, "I am the LORD your God" (Exodus 20:2).

### The Historical Prologue

The history leading to the cutting of the covenant was recited to prove the right of the superior party to make it. In the Ten Commandments, for example, the summary is simply, "... who brought you out of Egypt, out of the land of slavery" (Exodus 20:2).

### Requirements (Commandments)

The Torah contains 613 of the requirements God placed on the people with whom He was in relationship. He placed even more obligations on Himself. In summarizing the commandments, these requirements were simplified to ten (Exodus 20:3–17). Some scholars have noted that Jesus reduced His summary to just two obligations (Matthew 22:37–40).

### Blessings and Curses

Keeping a covenant brought specific rewards, and breaking it brought specific penalties. The Torah, for example, contains many blessings and curses.

### The Summary Document

The short summary document, which could be easily read and stored, summarized the entire covenant and so represented the total relationship between the parties. Normally in Near Eastern culture, two summary documents were made; each party kept one in a sacred place. So, it seems clear that each tablet of the Ten Commandments contained all of the commandments. One copy was God's, and the other belonged to the people of Israel. Part of the purpose of the ark of the covenant was to hold the Ten Commandments, the summary of God's covenant with His people.

# additional Resources

### History

Connolly, Peter. *Living in the Time of Jesus of Nazareth.* Tel Aviv: Steimatzky, 1983.

Ward, Kaari. *Jesus and His Times.* New York: Reader's Digest, 1987.

Whiston, William, trans. *The Works of Josephus: Complete and Unabridged.* Peabody, Mass.: Hendrikson Publishers, 1987.

Wood, Leon. Revised by David O'Brien. *A Survey of Israel's History.* Grand Rapids: Zondervan, 1986.

### Jewish Roots of Christianity

Stern, David H. *Jewish New Testament Commentary.* Clarksville, Md.: Jewish New Testament Publications, 1992.

Wilson, Marvin R. *Our Father Abraham: Jewish Roots of the Christian Faith.* Grand Rapids: Eerdmans, 1986.

Young, Brad H. *Jesus the Jewish Theologian.* Peabody, Mass.: Hendrickson Publishers, 1995.

### Geography

Beitzel, Barry J. *The Moody Atlas of Bible Lands.* Chicago: Moody Press, 1993.

Gardner, Joseph L. *Reader's Digest Atlas of the Bible.* New York: Reader's Digest, 1993.

### General Background

Alexander, David, and Pat Alexander, eds. *Eerdmans' Handbook to the Bible.* Grand Rapids: Eerdmans, 1983.

Butler, Trent C., ed. *Holman Bible Dictionary.* Nashville: Holman Bible Publishers, 1991.

Edersheim, Alfred. *The Life and Times of Jesus the Messiah.* Peabody, Mass.: Hendrickson Publishers, 1994.

### Archaeological Background

Charlesworth, James H. *Jesus Within Judaism: New Light from Exciting Archaeological Discoveries.* New York: Doubleday, 1988.

Finegan, Jack. *The Archaeology of the New Testament: The Life of Jesus and the Beginning of the Early Church.* Princeton: Princeton University Press, 1978.

Mazar, Amihai. *Archaeology of the Land of the Bible: 10,000–586 B.C.E.* New York: Doubleday, 1990.

To learn more about the specific backgrounds of the fourth set of videos, consult the following resources:

Avigad, Nahman. "Jerusalem in Flames—The Burnt House Captures a Moment in Time." *Biblical Archaeology Review* (November–December 1983).

Barkey, Gabriel. "The Garden Tomb—Was Jesus Buried Here?" *Biblical Archaeology Review* (March–April 1986).

Ben Dov, Meir. "Herod's Mighty Temple Mount." *Biblical Archaeology Review* (November–December 1986).

Bivin, David. "The Miraculous Catch." *Jerusalem Perspective* (March–April 1992).

Burrell, Barbara, Kathryn Gleason, and Ehud Netzer. "Uncovering Herod's Seaside Palace." *Biblical Archaeology Review* (May–June 1993).

Edersheim, Alfred. *The Temple*. London: James Clarke & Co., 1959.

Edwards, William D., Wesley J. Gabel, and Floyd E. Hosmer. "On the Physical Death of Jesus Christ." *Journal of American Medical Association (JAMA)* (March 21, 1986).

Flusser, David. "To Bury Caiaphas, Not to Praise Him." *Jerusalem Perspective* (July–October 1991).

Greenhut, Zvi. "Burial Cave of the Caiaphas Family." *Biblical Archaeology Review* (September–October 1992).

Hareuveni, Nogah. *Nature in Our Biblical Heritage*. Kiryat Ono, Israel: Neot Kedumim, Ltd., 1980.

Hepper, F. Nigel. *Baker Encyclopedia of Bible Plants: Flowers and Trees, Fruits and Vegetables, Ecology*. Ed. by J. Gordon Melton. Grand Rapids: Baker, 1993.

"The 'High Priest' of the Jewish Quarter." *Biblical Archaeology Review* (May–June 1992).

Hirschfeld, Yizhar, and Giora Solar. "Sumptuous Roman Baths Uncovered Near Sea of Galilee." *Biblical Archaeology Review* (November–December 1984).

Hohlfelder, Robert L. "Caesarea Maritima: Herod the Great's City on the Sea." *National Geographic* (February 1987).

Holum, Kenneth G. *King Herod's Dream: Caesarea on the Sea*. New York: W. W. Norton, 1988.

Mazar, Benjamin. "Excavations Near Temple Mount Reveal Splendors of Herodian Jerusalem." *Biblical Archaeology Review* (July–August 1980).

Nun, Mendel. *Ancient Stone Anchors and Net Sinkers from the Sea of Galilee*. Israel: Kibbutz Ein Gev, 1993. (Also available from *Jerusalem Perspective*.)

_____. "Fish, Storms, and a Boat." *Jerusalem Perspective* (March–April 1990).

_____. "The Kingdom of Heaven Is Like a Seine." *Jerusalem Perspective* (November–December 1989).

_____. "Net Upon the Waters: Fish and Fishermen in Jesus' Time." *Biblical Archaeology Review* (November–December 1993).

_____. *The Sea of Galilee and Its Fishermen in the New Testament*. Israel: Kibbutz Ein Gev, 1993. (Also available from *Jerusalem Perspective*.)

Pileggi, David. "A Life on the Kinneret." *Jerusalem Perspective* (November–December 1989).

Pixner, Bargil. *With Jesus Through Galilee According to the Fifth Gospel*. Rosh Pina, Israel: Corazin Publishing, 1992.

Pope, Marvin, H. "Hosanna: What It Really Means." *Bible Review* (April 1988).

Riech, Ronny. "Ossuary Inscriptions from the Caiaphas Tomb." *Jerusalem Perspective* (July–October 1991).

_____. "Six Stone Water Jars." *Jerusalem Perspective* (July–September 1995).

Ritmeyer, Kathleen. "A Pilgrim's Journey." *Biblical Archaeology Review* (November–December 1989).

Ritmeyer, Kathleen, and Leen Ritmeyer. "Reconstructing Herod's Temple Mount in Jerusalem." *Biblical Archaeology Review* (November–December 1989).

_____. "Reconstructing the Triple Gate." *Biblical Archaeology Review* (November–December 1989).

Ritmeyer, Leen. "The Ark of the Covenant: Where It Stood in Solomon's Temple." *Biblical Archaeology Review* (January–February 1996).

_____. "Quarrying and Transporting Stones for Herod's Temple Mount." *Biblical Archaeology Review* (November–December 1989).

Sarna, Nahum M. *The JPS Torah Commentary: Exodus.* New York: Jewish Publication Society, 1991.

"Sea of Galilee Museum Opens Its Doors." *Jerusalem Perspective* (July–September 1995).

Shanks, Hershel. "Excavating in the Shadow of the Temple Mount." *Biblical Archaeology Review* (November–December 1986).

"Shavuot." *Encyclopedia Judaica,* Volume 14. Jerusalem: Keter Publishing House, 1980.

Stern, David. *Jewish New Testament Commentary.* Clarksville, Md.: Jewish New Testament Publications, 1992.

Taylor, Joan E. "The Garden of Gethsemane." *Biblical Archaeology Review* (July–August 1995).

Tzaferis, Vassilios. "Crucifixion—The Archaeological Evidence." *Biblical Archaeology Review* (January–February 1985).

_____. "A Pilgrimage to the Site of the Swine Miracle." *Biblical Archaeology Review* (March–April 1989).

_____. "Susita." *Biblical Archaeology Review* (September–October 1990).

Vann, Lindley. "Herod's Harbor Construction Recovered Underwater." *Biblical Archaeology Review* (May–June 1983).

# transform your life through a journey of discovery into the world of the Bible

## Faith Lessons Video Series
### *Ray Vander Laan*

Filmed on location in Israel, **Faith Lessons** is a unique video series that brings God's Word to life with astounding relevance. By weaving together the Bible's fascinating historical, cultural, religious, and geographical contexts, teacher and historian Ray Vander Laan reveals keen insights into Scripture's significance for modern believers. These illuminating "faith lessons" afford a new understanding of the Bible that will ground your convictions and transform your life.

The **Faith Lessons** video series is ideal for use at home, especially in personal and family Bible studies. Individual believers and families will gain vital insights from long ago times and cultures through this innovative approach to Bible study.

> *"Nothing has opened and illuminated the Scriptures for me quite like the Faith Lessons series."*
>
> —Dr. James Dobson

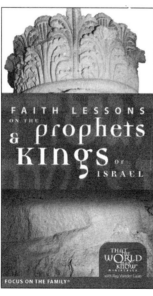

**Faith Lessons on the Promised Land**
*Crossroads of the World*
**Volume One**
0-310-67864-1

**Faith Lessons on the Prophets & Kings of Israel**
**Volume Two**
0-310-67865-X

**Faith Lessons on the Life & Ministry of the Messiah**
**Volume Three**
0-310-67866-8

**Faith Lessons on the Death & Resurrection of the Messiah**
**Volume Four**
0-310-67867-6

# travel back in time to see the sights, hear the sounds, and experience the wonder of Jesus— all through the power of interactive CD-ROM.

## Jesus
### *An Interactive Journey*

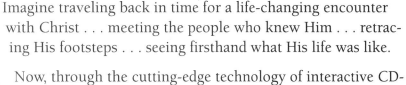

Imagine traveling back in time for a life-changing encounter with Christ . . . meeting the people who knew Him . . . retracing His footsteps . . . seeing firsthand what His life was like.

Now, through the cutting-edge technology of interactive CD-ROM, you can make that incredible voyage—back to the life and times of Jesus! This exciting multimedia adventure takes you there, giving you an entirely new appreciation for the fascinating historical, geographical, and cultural backdrop that will enhance your understanding of the Gospel.

An innovative "Visitor's Center" is your gateway to more than 180 different avenues of study, from Christ's birth to His resurrection. With a click of the mouse, you'll be guided to dozens of colorful locales, where you'll experience through the eyes and ears of ancient Jews and Romans what Christ's world was really like.

Or take a self-guided tour and stroll at your own pace through the lively marketplace to learn about trade and commerce, pause to listen in on the people, or go to the synagogue to gain a better understanding of the religious practices of the day.

The high technology and vast amount of material in this unique presentation will captivate you for hours, while providing a solid understanding of the Gospel and its relevance to today's believer. It's great for personal and family Bible study, Christian schools, and a wide variety of church uses.

*Compatible with Windows® 95 and Windows® 3.1*

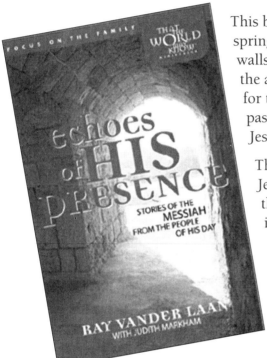